# SWARMWISE

*The Tactical Manual to Changing the World*

## RICK FALKVINGE

This is version 1.1 (first edition, second revision) of *Swarmwise*. The differences from the first print revision are mostly cosmetic.

You are free to make as many copies of this book as you like and share with friends and strangers, as long as you credit the author and you don't sell them. Actually, you're not just *free* to share copies with your friends, but downright *encouraged* to. If you like this book, why shouldn't you share it with your friends?

**ISBN-10:** 1463533152

**ISBN-13:** 9781463533151

Library of Congress Control Number : 2013909028

CreateSpace Publishing Platform, North Charleston, SC

"Your most valuable asset isn't your employees,"
I told the executive.

"Your most valuable asset is the thousands of
people who want to work for you for free, and
you don't let them."

# SMARMWISE CONTENTS

## PART I: BUILDING THE SWARM

## PART II: LEADING THE SWARM

## PART III: DELIVERING WITH THE SWARM

## APPENDICES ETC.

*December 29, 2005, in the afternoon, about tea time.*

*I call my old friend Rickard "Richie" Olsson, who has known my entre-preneurial spirit for a long time. We even shared an apartment once, a long time ago, where he was subjected to my wild ideas on a daily basis. I have this new idea and want him to be the first person to know about it and give me his reaction to it.*

*"Hey, Richie, you know that project that went wild a while back? I've been thinking of something. I may have a new project in the works here that can potentially take on quite a high profile — higher than, say, the Pirate Bay."*

*A heavy sigh is heard on the other end.*

*"What has gotten into your mind this time?"*

# PART I

---

## BUILDING
## THE
## SWARM

# CHAPTER ONE

# Understanding the Swarm

Somewhere today, a loose-knit group of activists who are having fun is dropkicking a rich, established organization so hard they are making heads spin. Rich and resourceful organizations are used to living by the golden rule — "those with the gold make the rules." New ways of organizing go beyond just breaking the old rules into downright shredding them — leaving executives in the dust, wondering how that band of poor, ragtag, disorganized activists could possibly have beaten their rich, well-structured organization.

On June 7, 2009, the Swedish Pirate Party got 225,915 votes in the European elections, becoming the largest party in the most coveted subthirty demographic. Our campaign budget was fifty thousand euros. Our competitors had spent six million. We had spent less than 1 percent of their budget and still beat them, giving us a cost-efficiency advantage of *over two orders of magnitude*. This was entirely due to working *swarmwise*, and the methods can translate to almost any organized large-scale activity. This book is about that secret sauce.

A swarm organization is a decentralized, collaborative effort of volunteers that looks like a hierarchical, traditional organization from the outside. It is built by a small core of people that construct a scaffolding of go-to people, enabling a large number of volunteers to cooperate on a common goal in quantities of people not possible before the net was available.

Working with a swarm requires you to do a lot of things completely opposite from what you learn at an archetypal business school. You need to release the control of your brand and its messages. You need to delegate authority to the point where anybody can make almost any decision for the entire organization. You need to accept and embrace that people in the organization will do exactly as they please, and the only way to lead is to inspire them to want to go where you want the organization as a whole to go.

It is only as you release that control, the kind of control that organizations and managers have held close to heart for centuries, that you can reap the benefits of the swarm: the same cost-efficiency advantage and execution-speed advantage against the competition that the Swedish Pirate Party enjoyed. This book will teach you those methods, from the initial forming of the swarm to its growth and ongoing maintenance and delivery. It will not teach you the underlying theory of psychology and sociology — merely share experiences and methods that have been proven to work in practice.

When I kick-started the swarm of the Swedish Pirate Party, I had posted a rough manifesto on a rather ugly website and mentioned the site just once in a chat channel of a file-sharing lobby. That was all the advertising that ever happened; the next day, the party had hundreds of activists. Timing, social context, and message are crucial – but if you have those three, your initial swarm will form like bees to honey in hours. Growing it and maintaining it will also be crucial, but those are the next challenges in line. We take one challenge at a time.

As we describe the swarm concept, it is easy to think of pure decentralized amorphous clouds of people, like Anonymous or the Occupy Wall Street movement. However, while these swarms share *values*, they do not share *direction or method*. That means they are confined to succeeding on small projects that span a relatively small number of people over a relatively short time span, even if each of those small projects builds gradual awareness of the Anonymous or Occupy brands.

The weak cohesion of the Anonymous and Occupy brands can partially be ascribed to their choice of being leaderless. While this brings resilience, as no leader can be targeted by adversaries, it sacrifices direction and purpose. I've found that the typical Internet community methods of inclusion, when combined with strong leadership, work much better to achieve global change than working leaderlessly under little more than a common flag.

I learned some of these techniques while being trained for officer's rank in the army, and even more of them by participating in many online communities. But the secret sauce recipe of swarm cost efficiency was hit only when I took an officer's training in maintaining strong group values, mixed in the net's strong participatory values and low-cost mass communication, and added a dash of management experience from the dot-com era at the turn of the century.

That dot-com era was quite special as a manager in the IT field. If your people didn't like what you said at the morning meeting, they would merrily walk out of the building and have a new job before lunch. Your paycheck was far more replaceable to them than they ever were as employees to you. People didn't work for the money.

Therefore, this experience carries over directly to working with volunteers, where people don't work for the money either (as they aren't getting any). Leadership and positive reinforcement are key.

Perhaps most significantly, focus in the swarm is always on what everybody *can* do, and never what people *cannot* or *must* do.

 Focus in the swarm is always on what everybody can do.

This sets it completely apart from a traditional corporation or democratic institution, which focuses sharply on what people *must* do and what bounds and limits they are *confined to*. This difference is part of why a swarm can be so effective: everybody can find something he or she likes to do, all the time, off a suggested palette that furthers the swarm's goals — and there is nobody there to tell people how things must or may not be done.

Rather, people inspire one another. There are no report lines among activists. As everybody communicates with everybody else all the time, successful projects quickly create ripples to other parts of the swarm. Less successful ones cause the swarm to learn and move on, with no fingers pointed.

If you want leadership in a swarm, you stand up and say, *"I'm going to do X, because I think it will accomplish Y. Anybody who wants to join me in doing X is more than welcome."* Anybody in the swarm can stand up and say this, and everybody is encouraged to. This quickly creates an informal but tremendously strong leadership structure where people seek out roles that maximize their impact in furthering the swarm's goals — all happening organically without any central planning and organizational charts.

 A swarm is led from the front lines. People who take initiatives usually get them.

At the bottom line, what sets a swarm apart from traditional organizations is its blinding speed of operation, its next-to-nothing operating costs, and its large number of very devoted volunteers. Traditional corporations and democratic institutions appear to work at *glacial* speeds from the inside of a swarm. That's also why a swarm can change the world: it runs circles around traditional organizations in terms of quality and quantity of work, as well as in resource efficiency.

## THE SWARM IS OPEN...

A key aspect of the swarm is that it is open to all people who want to share in the workload. Actually, it is more than open — everybody in the whole world is *encouraged* to pick work items off a public list, without asking anybody's permission, and just start doing them. There is no recruitment process. Anybody who wants to contribute to the goal, in his or her own way and according to his or her own capacity, is welcome to do so. This contrasts sharply with hiring processes at traditional organizations, where people have to pass some kind of test in order to start working for the organization.

The advantage of this approach is that resources of the swarm aren't spent keeping people *out* of it, but are spent getting people *in* to it. Granted, some work will be a duplication of effort since many people will be working on the same thing when nobody gets to tell other people what to do — but the result will be several solutions that are tried in parallel, and the swarm quickly learns which solutions work and which don't. The workflow becomes an iterative, evolutionary process of trial and error, of constantly adapting and improving, without anybody's supervision to make it happen.

Being open and inviting is a key defining feature of a swarm.

## ...AND TRANSPARENT

The swarm isn't just open, it is also *transparent* as a defining feature. There are almost no secrets at all. This can be a mind-boggling concept, coming from a traditional organization.

Everything is transparent by default. Financial records are transparent for all to see. Discussions about strategies and tactics are transparent for all to see (and open for all to participate in). Conflicts are transparent for all to see. This is because all discussions happen in places where everyone can see them.

This provides for trust and confidence. Since everybody can see all the information and all the discussions in the entire organization, it provides a very powerful sense of inclusion.

It also provides an extremely effective rumor control. It is an inoculation against distrust, since distrust depends on information starvation and people drawing their own conclusions from incomplete data.

Transparency is also effective at preventing scandalization: there have been several instances in the Swedish Pirate Party where media caught wind of a conflict and sensationalized it in a typical tabloid fashion, at which point a normal organization would have capsized — but since everybody reading the stories was able to go to the source and read the actual and original exchange of words, there were no rumors, and there was no "he said, she said." Conflicts do not escalate beyond control when this transparency is in place.

Of course, this doesn't mean every discussion over coffee or a drink must be recorded. That would create an untenable workload, and couldn't be enforced anyway. But it does mean that work isn't applied to keep some people away from information that is available to other people — so when discussions are held online, they remain recorded and they remain readable.

> "BEWARE OF HE WHO WOULD DENY YOU ACCESS TO INFORMATION, FOR IN HIS HEART, HE DREAMS HIMSELF YOUR MASTER."
> — *COMMISSIONER PRAVIN LAL*

In the few cases where secrets are kept, they are to protect the privacy of people in the swarm, and anybody can easily find exactly what information is kept secret — and, more importantly, *why* it is kept secret and who has the knowledge of it.

An example of a legitimate secret in a swarm could be the identities of donors, in order to protect the donors and prevent conflicts of interest as people would consciously or subconsciously try to please the larger donors rather than work toward the overall goal of the swarm. The person administering the bank account and/or credit card records would know this, but would be tasked with keeping it to himself or herself.

Last but not least, being fully transparent alleviates the problem in traditional chain-of-command structures where somebody in the middle may distort information passed up or down, either consciously or subconsciously, in the scenario where every link in the chain is an information bottleneck. By making all the information available to everybody, nobody will have the ability to distort it to parts of the organization. Conversely, nobody speaks for other people in a swarm, as everybody has his or her own voice. This prevents factionalization, as there aren't any traditional middle managers who can set their own goals that conflict with those of the overall swarm.

## SO YOU HAVE A PROVOCATIVE IDEA?

You are probably reading this book because you have one or a couple of provocative ideas lurking in the back of your head and are looking for ways to realize them. Here, then, comes the boring part of realizing them: have you done the math?

All swarms are a matter of quantity. Quantity of *people*. Like army ants in the Amazon rainforest, it is a matter of overpowering your opponents with *sheer biomass* through superior ability of organization and ability to channel volunteer energy — using your organizational agility to always be immensely stronger than your adversaries, whenever and wherever you choose to appear, just like the army ants overpower an opponent by their ability to quickly direct and relocate their local biomass advantage.

So this is the first hurdle your idea must pass: Are enough people affected by this idea, and can a large enough number of people be energized to contribute to it in order to pass the critical threshold? Can the threshold be identified, and, if so, how many people must get onboard for your idea to succeed?

As we can see, this is where it gets a bit traditional. We must determine what the success criterion for the idea is. What event *constitutes success,* and what does it take to get there?

For a new political party like the Swedish Pirate Party, the success criterion is easy to determine: *get elected.* There are many small steps on the road there, of course, and many steps after that goal has been achieved (such as *staying* elected). But it gives us a tangible goal to work with.

Let's see how this goal breaks down.

We would need activists in quality and voters in quantity. Politics, after all, is strictly a numbers game. It is a spectator sport performed in public.

In the case of the Pirate Party, the trigger for quantity was file sharing. In 2006, about 1.2 million citizens — *voters* — in Sweden were sharing culture and knowledge in violation of the copyright monopoly and didn't see anything wrong with that, but were still being actively demonized by the establishment.

To get into Parliament, you need 225,000 votes. This meant that if just one-fourth of the people thus demonized were angry enough about it and didn't take that kind of treatment sitting down, then the Pirate Party would be in Parliament. That was our goal, posted on the very first day on the website: 225,000 votes. It was credible, it was tangible, it was inclusive, it was world changing.

Of course, there were other factors in society to this conflict as well, the underlying themes being freedoms of speech and expression as well as general net liberties. But if you start talking about abstract concepts, you'll just have yawns among your prospective volunteers. We'll need a large recruitment surface with concepts that are easy to relate to people's everyday lives in order to grow the swarm to critical mass.

Once inside the swarm, people and activists will strive to understand the concepts on a deeper level. We need that, too. But the surface area of the swarm's idea must be large enough to attain the sufficient quantity of people for success.

Your idea must be possible to break down into that kind of math. How many people engaged at a minimum level, equivalent to voting, buying a product, or signing a petition, do you need to succeed?

You need to identify the group of people affected in a positive direction by your provocative idea, estimate the size of that group, and then make an educated guesstimate as to what portion of this group may engage in the swarm at the lowest level of activation.

However, remember the scale of the quantities of people we're talking about. Swarms typically engage hundreds of thousands of people, even millions. They're operated and coordinated by some thousand people who contribute to the swarm in their spare time, and maybe — just maybe — there are one or two full-time people coordinating the bulk of it.

Your swarm may have lower requirements for success than engaging one million people, of course. Only you can know that. But at least, you need to take your best guess at the numbers.

This is hard, because best guesses are all you'll ever get. For instance, a women's rights party in Sweden — which is already among the most gender-equal countries in the world — potentially affects a full half of the voter base. But can you activate a large enough portion of those people on the idea of further equalization of the genders? (It was tried. It turned out that you couldn't.)

In contrast, three years after launch, in 2009, the Swedish Pirate Party got 225,915 votes in the European elections, securing its first seats. The math had checked out beautifully from my initial estimate of 225,000 votes.

So for the rest of this book, we are going to take a hard look at your idea of how to form a swarm and see what is required to realize it, the way the Swedish Pirate Party realized its success and started changing the world.

We'll start with looking at the launch moments of the swarm, and see how intense they can be, and discuss how a scaffolding of go-to people — *officers* — can be organized in order to enable the swarm all across the ground you intend to cover. We'll be discussing techniques and methods for the swarm itself, even going down to practical things like handing out flyers and how you teach people to hand out flyers effectively.

Going from there, we'll take a closer look at how you can manage the day-to-day operations of the swarm — one portion classic project management, one large portion of wisdom about conflict resolution, and one portion of methods on preserving the swarm's goals, culture, and values as it grows.

Finally, we'll take a look at how you use the resulting swarm organization to deliver those large-scale results that change the world, as well as what happens when you succeed *too well*.

But first things first. Let's return to that provocative idea of yours, lurking in the back of your head, and discuss how we can begin realizing it.

*January 1, 2006, at 8:30 p.m. Central European Time.*

*Having worked with the Pirate Party website in my available spare time over the holidays, tomorrow will be an ordinary workday, and this New Year's Day is coming to a close. I wrap up my work on the site, replace anything nonfinished with the text "Placeholder," and take it online.*

*Having taken the very rudimentary site online, I choose to announce it carefully with little visibility. To test the waters, I go into the chat lobby of the file-sharing hub Ancient Spirit, where I'm nowhere near a regular, and write two lines:*

*"Hey, look, the Pirate Party has its website up after New Year's. http://www.piratpartiet.se/"*

*Looking at the web server, I see the first wave of visitors come immediately on my chat lines, maybe a dozen. Then comes a trickle of secondary visitors, people alerted to my initiative by the first wave. The first electronic signatures supporting the party's formal registration come in. After thirty signatures and another two hours, I feel I have to be happy with the launch, take a complete backup, and go to sleep for tomorrow's workday.*

*Things escalated quickly overnight through word of mouth without me being aware of it.*

*The next day, as I come in to work on January 2, I don't have many hours of the workday morning behind me as I read a message on a Mensa mailing list I follow: "Don't we know this Rick Falkvinge fellow that the newspapers are writing about today?"*

*I feel my eyes blinking in disbelief. Wait, what? "That the newspapers are writing about?"*

# CHAPTER TWO

# Launching Your Swarm

Launching a swarm is an intense event, where you can get hundreds or thousands of new colleagues in less than a day. You have a very short window for appreciating their interest, or they will take it elsewhere.

OK, so you have a provocative idea. You've done the math. Everything appears good to go. How do you gather a swarm around the idea?

A traditional method would be to go about an advertising campaign to generate interest. Working swarmwise, though, two words about the idea of an advertising campaign: *forget it.* If your idea doesn't generate enthusiasm on its own, no amount of whitewashing is going to create the grassroots activism that you need to form a swarm.

On the other hand, a swarm will form as long as you present a com-
pelling enough idea that people feel that they can be part of. You
don't need to spend ten million on an advertising campaign. It can
be enough to mention the idea just once in passing in a semiobscure
chat channel.

To traditional marketers, this sounds ridiculous. But that's what I
did to kick-start a brand that's now well known in the IT sector
worldwide and has local presence in seventy-plus countries.

When I started the Pirate Party in Sweden, I took its website online
and wrote two lines in a file-sharing hub's lobby chat. This was on
January 1, 2006, at 20:30 CET.

*Hey, look, the Pirate Party has its website up after New Year's.*
*http://www.piratpartiet.se/*

The site had a manifesto which was rough and unpolished, but
which came across as credible, tangible, inclusive, and world changing. The site itself was just as rough and unpolished — which is the
typical swarm way of trial and error, of putting a stake in the
ground and evolving from there:

And that's it. Those two lines announcing the rough-looking site are all the advertising I ever did. The next two days, the site got three million hits. (Sweden has nine million people.) The media caught on quickly, too. Worldwide. On the third day, my photo was in a Pakistani paper.

 Your idea needs to be tangible, credible, inclusive, and epic.

My point here is, if you're thinking hard about how to gather a swarm for your idea: don't worry about advertising.

Word of mouth is much more efficient than any campaign can ever be, but that requires that your idea — or rather, your presentation of it — meet four criteria: tangible, credible, inclusive, and epic.

**Tangible:** You need to post an outline of the goals you intend to meet, when, and how.

**Credible:** After having presented your daring goal, you need to present it as totally doable. Bonus points if nobody has done it before.

**Inclusive:** There must be room for participation by every spectator who finds it interesting, and they need to realize this on hearing about the project.

**Epic:** Finally, you must set out to change the entire world for the better — or at least make a major improvement for a lot of people.

If these four steps are good, then the swarm will form by itself. Quite rapidly, in the twenty-odd cases I have observed firsthand. *Very* rapidly. On the other hand, if these four components are not good enough, no amount of advertising or whitewashing is going to create the volunteer activist power that you want.

Let's take a look at sample project plans. I've seen many examples of all of these three types.

## A BAD EXAMPLE OF A PROJECT PLAN

Oh boy I am so starting a new project t0talli for Das Lulz!!11!!! oneone!!six!!11 lololol.

I wonder what I will put in it?

## ANOTHER EQUALLY BAD EXAMPLE

We are seeking a synergy between results-oriented actitivies related to dynamic business intelligence and competitive social media. Particularly, we are pursuing a path of cost-efficient achievements in quality predictability and static client satisfaction, measured by coupons used and referrals given. The means of achieving synergy is to strive for interaction with consumer focus groups in the field of cross-brand social communication and with student specialist groups in a study of networking revenue potential. The goal of the project is to raise the quarterly operating profits by up to 2 percent.

## A BETTER EXAMPLE

We will dropkick the politicians' worldwide war against online anonymity by deploying one million anonymizing TOR exit nodes and get the corresponding TOR client into the default-install codebase of at least 25 percent of browsers used worldwide by user count.

We will do this in seven stages, increasing the number of TOR exit nodes by a factor of five every sixty days. One stage of installed exit nodes will commit to recruiting five of their friends for the next stage of exit nodes to change the world in this manner. We will provide worldwide network recognition for the best contributors.

Halfway through the project, in stage four, we get the developers of the Firefox and Chrome web browsers to include the TOR client by default in their code base. If completed for deployment by stage five, everybody who wants to can be completely anonymous ever after.

We are going to change the world for the better and make it impossible for the stone age politicians to put the cat back in the bag. Want to be onboard for first stage of signups? Sign up HERE (link).

Now, we need to go back to our goals here. We want to gather tens of thousands of energized activists around an idea to change the world. Having an idea is not enough; the idea and its plan must energize people.

So don't worry about advertising. Mention your idea and plan in a couple of places where your intended activists would typically hang out. That's enough. If it's good, people will pick it up and talk to their friends in turn. It snowballs very quickly from there. If it doesn't energize, no advertising is going to change that.

If your idea is good and people can contribute, change the world, and see how it can be done, then you will have the first wave of hundreds of volunteers in less than a day. You will see hundreds of people holding out their hands, palms up, toward you and saying, "Here, use my hands! I want to be a part of this! Give me something to do!" in the electronic channels where you announce your presence.

The idea doesn't need to be polished. The important thing is to put that stake in the ground, start attracting people, and start working your way to the goal. In this, too much effort spent polishing the *appearance* of the idea rather than its own merits can even be counterproductive, as people can perceive it as glossed-over corporate whitewash.

This brings us to the next problem: taking care of these hundreds of people while they're still interested. They all will turn to you, personally, and there's just no way you will be physically able to give them all instructions on a one-to-one basis.

## SURVIVING THE INITIAL IMPACT

When your initiative hits the ground, and it is interesting enough to create a splash, then that splash will be unlike anything you have seen before. It can happen in many ways — it can be entirely word of mouth, it can become a major story in oldmedia, or, most commonly, it can hit the front page of one of many social news sites (or several of them at the same time).

When that happens, you will go from having been alone to suddenly having hundreds of people who want nothing more than to help you out on your project in their spare time. But their attention span is short; you need to respond. If you don't, they'll shrug and your initiative will wane out of memory in less than twenty-four hours.

In order to retain these hundreds of people, you also need a focal point for their interest — something as simple as a signup page or a forum. Of course, that focal point needs to be ready and functional when the impact of the idea hits, or the activists will be lost.

With the focal point active and the idea launched, it's said that one of the hardest steps you can take in a business is going from one person to two, as you recruit your first employee. When we're dealing with a swarm, everything is on a different scale. Here, we go from one person — you, the founder — to three hundred or more in the first instant.

It goes without saying that it can be a bit tricky, and you have at most twenty-four hours to sort out the situation or lose the initiative to form a swarm around this idea. What's worse, you can't really do it yourself. There is no way you can give individual and meaningful instructions to three hundred people in the attention span you have been given.

But the swarm can do it for you, if you let it. And you must.

The swarm's very first task will be to self-organize, and it excels at such tasks. But it is you who must set the structure and explicitly give the swarm the task to self-organize.

This is where traditional organizational theory kicks in to some degree.

Initially, you will be able to coordinate at most thirty groups, so create a discussion forum with at most that number of subgroups. You'll likely want to have people on streets and in squares campaigning for the swarm's cause before long, so subdividing your hatchling swarm by geography works well here — and when subdividing, create at most thirty subdivisions geographically. (Most countries have administrative divisions into counties, states, etc., that vary in number between fifteen and thirty units. If you're gunning for a Europe-wide movement, you can easily observe that the size of the EU plus a few hang-around countries fits the thirty-state limit well, and so on. The United States, with its fifty states, would be trickier, as would North America. Just pick a way to divide it into at most thirty units.)

Your discussion forum can take many forms. It can be a traditional web forum, it can be a wiki, it can be an etherpad, it can be any kind of collaborative space where people can go uninvited and just start working with others. I prefer the traditional forum because of its well-recognized form.

You'll need to make a judgment call on the approximate resulting group sizes, based on how many hands are at your disposal. Try to pick your geographical division so that the typical size is about seven members and no subgroup has more than thirty members. Don't announce this intent, as doing so would cause a distracting discussion about that action: just create the subgroups in a way that will cause this division to happen.

If you have more than a thousand people at your disposal in this initial splash, which can happen, then thirty subgroups of thirty people each will not be enough: that structure has a maximum of 30×30=900 people. In this rare case, you may need to exceed the thirty-people-per-group limit and have as many as 150 people each in thirty subgroups. This is a rare case, though, and you are not likely to encounter this.

(The magic numbers seven, thirty, and 150 are deeply integrated parts of the human social psyche — part of how we are wired. We'll return to how people behave in groups of those sizes in the next chapter.)

Having set the initial structure, you need to tell everybody to go to the appropriate subgroup and meet with other people who go there. Tell people to introduce themselves to one another, and to select a leader between them for the subgroup. At this point, you can safely refrain from giving instructions as to how that leader should be selected; the subgroups will come up with different ways that each have legitimacy in their respective group, and that's all that matters at this point.

No doubt, some subgroups will want to charge ahead here and figure out all the answers to life, the universe, and everything – but at this point, getting the basic structure in place is first priority, enabling further absorption of more activists into the swarm. You shouldn't tell people who charge ahead to hold and wait, though (more about this in later chapters); just make sure leaders get selected.

As leaders get picked by the subgroups, contact those leaders in person — at least a voice or video call, preferably over beer or coffee if you live nearby — and introduce yourself, and get to know them more personally. You'll be working closely with them in the near future, so you'll want to get a feel for them as people and colleagues, and to allow them to get a feel for who you are as a person and colleague.

You'll also want to set up a subforum where these subgroup leaders can discuss things between themselves and with you. Make sure that other people can read it. Don't keep secrets; rather, let everybody see the ongoing growth of your swarm.

This process takes a couple of days, but it kick-starts the swarm on all levels. You will have energized small subgroups of people who live reasonably close to each other, and they will have legitimate leaders — legitimate to them, anyway. The thirty leaders and you form an initial management team pyramid in the swarm's scaffolding of *officers*, the swarm's go-to people. Taken together, your subgroups form a comprehensive coverage of all the ground you intend to cover.

(A couple of weeks from this point, you will realize that you'll need an intermediate layer of officers in between you and these thirty — a few of them will have lost interest and gone radio silent, and you won't have noticed, because thirty people are too many to keep track of to that level if they don't contact you. Therefore, you will want an intermediate layer of five or six people between you and these thirty as the swarm grows. But don't worry about that at this stage — that's for the next chapter, and a couple of weeks out.)

## THE SWARM'S FIRST TASK

As the swarm organizes into these subgroups by geography, it needs to be given a task immediately that allows it to jell properly. If you just tell people to go to a forum, they will lose interest in a week if nothing more happens. These are people who wanted to help the swarm succeed with the work of their own hands, remember?

So in order to make this organization set and settle, there needs to be something to be done right away. In the case of the Swedish Pirate Party, that task was to collect two thousand signatures from the public to support the party's registration with the Election Authority. It needs to be a task that looks challenging but is doable for some hundred people; it needs to be a task where you can provide for internal competition between the thirty-or-so geographic subdivisions that you have created; and it needs to be a task where everybody can see the clear benefit to the swarm upon its completion. In the case of a political party, registering it with the Election Authority was an obvious benefit that everybody realized; you'll need to have a similar task at hand that leads to such a goal.

What this does is cause the swarm to learn how to work together over the first four weeks or so of its existence, as this task is being carried out in a decentralized fashion. You should update the overall progress of the goal at least daily.

A swarm organization isn't first and foremost reporting lines between boxes on an org chart. A swarm organization is people who know other people and who choose to work together. Therefore, getting people to know other people should be an overarching goal of your activities at this point.

Do encourage people to meet, and be very clear that they should not make it formal. Do not meet in a protocolized formal meeting under any circumstance, but meet instead over beer, pizza, and laughs. Focus on creating opportunities for people to get to know people, and for new people to feel welcomed to the group.

Once such meetings become regular, it becomes even more important to make sure that newcomers feel welcome. One method of accomplishing this can be to start every meeting with an introductory round where people present themselves briefly along with some piece of trivia, such as the latest thing they downloaded or shared: "Hi, I'm Rick, forty. I'm mostly known here for setting up an ugly website. The most recent thing I downloaded was an

Ubuntu Linux release." Seeing everybody present himself or herself helps newcomers immensely, and it provides for a convenient framing for the newcomers to introduce themselves, as well as for the regulars to learn the newcomers' names. Also, the local leaders will need to pay particular attention to the newcomers in every meeting, personally welcoming them back to the next meeting.

The organization consists only of relationships between people. For every new relationship that is created, the organization grows.

 The organization consists only of relationships between people.

## DEALING WITH ATTENTION JUNKIES

As the swarm has its initial successes, a very small number of people will strive to join not because they sympathize with the swarm's goals, but because they crave and demand attention for themselves, and the visibility of the swarm seems to be able to provide this to them.

As the swarm is open, you cannot and should not try to keep these people out — but you can deny them the space and spotlights they crave. It can be hard to detect them, but one telltale sign is that these people will demand attention from you *personally* rather than trying to build the overall swarm with people who aren't as visible yet. You will also notice that they think very much in terms of rank and hierarchy, whereas other people will think in terms of getting stuff done and changing the world.

A few particularly tricky people will work for the swarm's goals very hard for the first couple of weeks, and then use the built-up credibility to cash in on attention. As this happens, the transparency of the swarm is the best conceivable antidote, as such people typically depend on other people not comparing the different versions of the story they're being told.

This part of building a swarm is inevitable, it is tough to deal with, but you can rest assured that as long as you keep the swarm open and transparent, these kinds of people won't be able to hijack it for their own personal visibility. They will eventually flush themselves out, sometimes in quite a bit of disruption.

*January 2, 2006, in the afternoon.*

*After lunch, my boss, the CEO, hands me a cordless phone. "Rick, for you. It's Mia," he says. Mia? I think. I don't know any Mia.*

*"Rick Falkvinge? Hi. This is Mia Carron, with the Aftonbladet newspaper (one of Sweden's largest). We understand you're the man behind the new Pirate Party that everybody's talking about today," the voice says.*

*My mind goes blank. Aftonbladet? Calling me? … What was it that she said, "everybody's talking about"? I regain enough composure to realize I can't talk about this at work, but I might leave a little early today. "Can I call you back at 3 p.m.?" I ask.*

*Said and done. On my way home from work, my first interview happens, taking me completely aback.*

*"Are you the party leader?" the reporter asks.*

*"Uhm, I guess so...," I hear myself respond. "I'm not really used to that title."*

*As I arrive home from work that day, the interview has already been published online in the newspaper Aftonbladet, alongside an online poll. Sixty-one percent of the respondents in the poll say they can see themselves voting for the Pirate Party. We need 4 percent to succeed. Over fifty thousand people have already responded, so it is not just statistical noise. I feel the rush of adrenaline sharpen my senses.*

*The game is on.*

# CHAPTER THREE

# Getting Your Swarm Organized: Herding Cats

While the effective swarm consists almost entirely of loosely knit activists, there is a core of people — a scaffolding for the swarm — that requires a more formal organization. It is important to construct this scaffolding carefully, paying attention to known facts about how people work in social groups. Without it, the swarm has no focal point around which it can... well, swarm.

If the last chapter was about the first six to eight days of the swarm's lifecycle, this chapter is about the first six to eight weeks.

In building this scaffolding of go-to people, of the swarm's *officers*, it is your responsibility to be aware of limits to group sizes that prevent further growth once reached, and break up the groups that reach these sizes into smaller subgroups when that happens.

You also need to be aware that any organization copies the methods and culture of its founder. This means that the swarm will do exactly as you do, regardless of persistent attempts to teach them good manners. The only way to have the swarm behave well is to behave well yourself. We'll be returning to this observation later in this chapter.

## THE THREE MAGIC GROUP SIZES

The few people upholding the scaffolding of the swarm will resemble a traditional hierarchical organization. However, it is important to understand that the role of this scaffolding is not directing and controlling the masses, as it would be in a corporation or other traditional organization. Rather, its role and value is in *supporting* the other 95 percent of the organization — the swarm — which makes its own decisions based on the values you communicate and looks to the scaffolding only when assistance, support, or resources are needed.

Nevertheless, to build an efficient scaffolding, we must understand the human psyche when it comes to optimal group sizes and organizational theory.

It can be easily observed in any organization that working groups larger than seven people fragment into two smaller groups. There are several theories as to why this happens, but the prevailing theory has to do with the amount of effort we need to spend upholding and caring for relationships within a working group. Let's illustrate with an example.

In a group of two people, there is just one relationship that the group needs to care for.

In a group of three people, there are three relationships (A to B, B to C, and A to C).

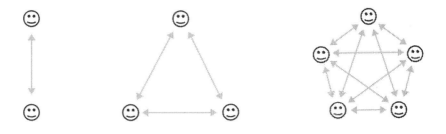

In a group of five, there are suddenly 4+3+2+1 = *ten* relationships. And if we up the group size to the critical seven people, there are *twenty-one* relationships between people that the group needs to maintain in order to function as a working group.

As we can see in this math, the social complexity of the group increases much faster than the group size. At some point, the group becomes inefficient, having to spend so much effort just on cohering the group that it gets very little or no actual work done.

When we add an eighth member to a group, the number of relationships to maintain climbs from twenty-one to twenty-eight. So while adding an eighth member to the group adds 14 percent work capacity to the group compared to seven people, it also requires the group to spend 33 percent more of their combined work capacity on the task of maintaining the group itself, on maintaining twenty-eight relationships instead of twenty-one. At this point, or sometimes at a ninth member, the group falls apart.

What we learn from this is that the scaffolding needs to be constructed so that no more than seven people work closely with one another in a given tight context.

We do this in the classical way, by constructing the scaffolding's organizational chart so that no person has more than six people working with him or her in a given context. This means that, for a given *geography* (like any state, country, city, etc.) in the organizational chart, that geography must subdivide into at most six smaller geographies which have other people responsible for those smaller geographies.

For now, we call this type of officer a *geography leader* for the swarm. He or she could be a state leader, city leader, circuit leader — any size of geography — but his or her duties will basically be the same.

(You will recall that we kick-started the swarm by subdividing it by geography and letting geography leaders emerge through self-organization.)

Also, for every geography, we will probably have four *function officers* and one or two *deputies* in addition to the geography leader. (We'll be returning to these terms and a sample organizational chart later in this chapter.) This, again, makes a group of at most seven in total.

So the key message here is that no geography leader should have more than six people working directly with him or her in a given context. This means that we construct a number of organizational mini-pyramids from the top down in the scaffolding, each with (at most) seven people in it, where each geography leader is both at the bottom of one pyramid and at the top of another, the one immediately below, as shown in this picture:

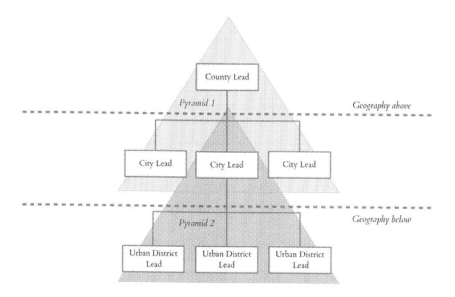

So the smallest of the three magic social group sizes is seven.

The largest is 150.

There is no relationship between these numbers. The number seven appears to come from a practical limit to the effort spent on maintaining a group, as previously explained. The more elusive number 150 appears to be a limit hardwired into our brains.

The number 150 appears in tons of places through human organizational history. It is our *maximum tribe size*. In a given context, we have the capacity to know this many people by name and have the loosest of bonds with them.

Anthropologists, looking at the size of the neocortex in our brain and comparing it to those of other primates and their tribe sizes, tend to regard this number as a biological limit.

This limit is also known as *Dunbar's Number,* or the *Dunbar Limit,* from British anthropologist Robin Dunbar, who first wrote about it.

If you are working at a company which has fewer than 150 employees, odds are that you know them all by name — or at least you have the capacity to do so. Beyond that size, you start referring to anonymous people by their *function* rather than referring to people you know by their name. You'll go see "somebody in Support," rather than "having a talk with Maria or Dave."

The most successful companies, organizations, and cultures are keenly aware of this human limit. To take the Amish as one example, as their settlements approach 150 in size, they split the settlement into two. The company Gore and Associates — more known as the makers of the Gore-Tex fabric — never puts more than 150 employees in a single plant. There are many more examples.

The effect on building your organization is the same as in every other successful organization: you need to know that groups above 150 people in size will lose the social bonding required for efficiency and, well, the *fun*.

However, you probably won't have any formal group of this size. Rather, it is the *informal* groups that inevitably form that you need to pay attention to, and how they — once they hit this limit — can prevent further growth of the swarm.

In particular, you need to pay attention to the initial and horizontal team of people that will gather in a chat channel or similar spot, probably titled "chat channel about everything related to the swarm." This organically formed group will have a glass ceiling of 150 people in size, and unless you are aware of these mechanisms, that glass ceiling won't be noticed. When this happens, further necessary growth of the swarm will be prevented, as more people can't be socially integrated into that initial chat channel.

Therefore, it is your task to make sure that there are social subswarms everywhere that can attract and retain new people, and not just one centrally located chat channel. These subswarms, too, will have that social maximum size of 150.

 When the swarm hits 150 people, you must start breaking it up into smaller groups.

Finally, the third magic group size is thirty. This is a group which falls between our tight working group and those we know by name, but not much more: we are capable of knowing more than just their names in the group of thirty, we know a couple of interests and curious facts about the others in this group, but we can't work tightly with all of them. It can be thought of as an extended family.

You will probably have a couple of formal groups that are about thirty people in size, like the assembled group of all officers and leaders for a certain function or geography, but in general, you should strive for the seven-person group. When looking at how several of these groups cooperate on a daily basis, if you notice that some groups cooperate more closely than others, you should be aware of the thirty-person group size limit. For example, if the group coordinating all the aspects of the work in a particular city starts approaching thirty-five people, then that group is blocking further growth of the swarm and should be divided into two, allowing for more growth: divided into two groups handling the north and south parts of the city, for example.

After reviewing this, we also realize why we divided the swarm by geography in chapter 2, and tried to have not more than thirty geographies. There's you, who founded the swarm, and you communicate directly with the (at most) thirty geography leaders.

If you did this, then three to four weeks into the swarm's lifecycle, it is suitable to insert a layer of officers between you and those thirty, so that you communicate directly with five or six newly inserted geography leaders, and they in turn communicate with five or six each of the original geography leaders.

So to summarize the important part of this: keep formal working groups in the scaffolding to about seven people. When several groups are working together, try to keep the size at or below thirty. Finally, pay close attention to when informal swarm groups approach 150 people in size. When that happens, take steps to break them up in smaller subgroups.

(I first learned of the different dynamics of these three group sizes — seven, thirty, and 150 — as part of my army officer's training in my early twenties. It is no coincidence that they correspond to squad, platoon, and company size, respectively. Since then, these group sizes have reappeared in almost every leadership training and management workshop, in one aspect or another. More importantly, all my experience with building swarms confirms their importance.)

## SELF-ORGANIZATION

All this talk about leaders and formal structure sounds very…*conventional,* doesn't it? We're building this thing called a scaffolding, but it sounds very much like a traditional, hierarchical, boring organization. So what is new?

The new part is the entire swarm *around* the scaffolding, and the role that these officers — these geographical and functional leaders — must take in order to support it.

One key insight is that the responsibility of the swarm leaders is not so much *managerial* as it is *janitorial.* Nobody answers to them, and their task is to make sure that the swarm has everything it needs to self-organize and work its miracles.

Remember, leadership in a swarm is received through inspiring others: standing up, doing without asking permission, and leading by example. In this task, the various officers and leaders have no organizational advantage over other people in the swarm: those who inspire others in a swarm cause things to happen.

Put another way, the leaders and officers are not somebody's boss just because they have some responsibility.

The first time you see people self-organize, it feels like magic. What you need to do is to communicate very clearly what you want to see happen and why. If people agree with you, they will make that happen, without you telling a single person what to do further. They will self-organize, and people interested in making it happen will gravitate by themselves to a subtask where they can help deliver the desired result. Each person will do this in his or her own way according to his or her own skill set, with no assignment or micro-supervision necessary, causing the whole of the task to happen.

This is also a key mechanism in swarm organizations. You cannot and should not try to tell anybody in the swarm what to do; rather, your role is to set goals and ambitions, ambitions that don't stop short of changing the entire world for the better.

We have seen something similar happen already, when the first onslaught of activists happened in chapter 2 and several hundred people were waiting for instructions. You told them to self-organize by geography and choose leaders for the geographies. That was a form of self-organization, albeit a rudimentary one.

In a swarm, working groups will form by themselves left and right to accomplish subtasks of your overall vision, subtasks you haven't even identified. This is part of how a swarm works and why it can be so effective.

So once the scaffolding of officers is in place, with its responsibility to support the swarm, groups and activities will form all over without any central planning — and, importantly, without any central control.

Your passion for the swarm's mission is going to be key in making this happen. You need to constantly show your passion for the end goal, and those who see and pick up on your passion will seek out things they can do to further it — all on their own.

Your role in this is to lead by example. People will copy you, in good weather and bad. Therefore, make sure you're being seen in good weather. More on this later.

Another thing you will notice as the self-organization starts to happen is that it doesn't necessarily follow geographical boundaries. This is fundamentally good; you will have groups that form around accomplishing specific tasks that are geographically unbound, as well as groups that form around tasks that are bound to a specific area by nature. The task of producing a press center isn't tied to a city, but the task of handing out flyers is. When people self-organize, this is taken care of by itself.

## ORG CHARTS AND ORGANIC GROWTH

There are three key concepts the swarm organization is optimized for: *speed*, *trust*, and *scalability*. When building the Swedish Pirate Party, this was a deliberate decision from the start, and it proved very successful.

We can optimize for *speed* by removing all conceivable bottlenecks. A swarm is typically starved of money, so it must compete on other grounds. Its reaction speed and reaction weight are more than enough to offset the lack of funds.

We can optimize for *trust* by keeping the swarm transparent and giving everybody a very far-reaching mandate to act on his or her own. We would establish this mandate by very clearly communicating that different people drive the swarm's goals in different ways, and that we all trust one another to do what he or she believes is best, even if we don't understand it ourselves. The three-activist rule, which we will discuss shortly, is a very efficient way to achieve this.

We can optimize for *scalability* by constructing the entire scaffolding at its finished size at the swarm's get-go, providing space in the organizational chart for everyone from geography leaders down to the neighborhood level. However, we would leave upwards of 99 percent of the roles in the scaffolding empty for now — below the original thirty geography leaders, nothing has been appointed yet, despite us having another six or seven layers of empty boxes in the scaffolding's organizational chart. This means that these geography leaders can and will grow the organization downward as activists volunteer to become new geography leaders at lower levels in the scaffolding. Then, those leaders will grow the organization in turn, and so on.

 A swarm optimizes for speed, trust, and scalability.

The first time you notice that somebody you've never heard of has been appointed to formal responsibility, it feels like magic, and it shows that the scaling-out is working.

A swarm grows by people who are talking to people at the individual activist level. You don't have the luxury of putting out ads, but your passion and desire to change the world for the better (along with a complete denial of what other people would call the impossibility of the task) make people talk among one another. This is how your swarm grows: one conversation at a time, one person at a time.

This is how the Swedish Pirate Party grew to fifty thousand members and eighteen thousand activists: one conversation at a time between passionate activists and potential new passionate activists.

In general, we can divide the people of the swarm into three groups by activity level: officers, activists, and passive supporters. The officers are the people in the scaffolding, people who have taken on the formal responsibility of upholding the swarm. Activists are the actual swarm, the people that make things happen on a huge scale. The passive supporters are people who agree with the goals as such, but haven't taken any action beyond possibly signing up for a mailing list or membership. (The passive supporters may sound less useful to the swarm, but that's not the case: they are the primary recruiting base for the next wave of activists. We'll discuss this more in chapter 8, as we look at the *Activation Ladder*.)

So let's take a look at what officers would typically be needed to support a swarm. In other words, let's look at a template organizational chart.

Let's take a typical geography as an example. It could be a county, it could be a city, it could be a state, doesn't matter. From the experience with the Swedish Pirate Party, we know that a particular geography works best when there is not just one geography leader, but a leader and a deputy who divide the work between themselves and who cover for one another. These people become go-to people for everything that happens in the area. The advantage of having two people is that people can drop out for a while from time to time. We can change jobs, we can fall madly in love, we can get sick, or we can lose interest in activism briefly for a myriad of other reasons. This is human, and always OK. If there are two people sharing the workload, the activity doesn't stop when one drops out for a while. Most geographies had one deputy geography leader, some had two.

"IF YOU FEEL YOU NEED TO TAKE A BREAK FROM ACTIVISM, THAT IS ALWAYS THE RIGHT THING TO DO. IT'S ALWAYS BETTER TO GET RESTED AND COME BACK THAN TO BURN OUT AND GET BITTER. THERE WILL ALWAYS BE SOMETHING TO DO WHEN YOU COME BACK: YOU DON'T HAVE TO WORRY ABOUT THE WORLD RUNNING OUT OF EVIL WHILE YOU'RE AWAY."

— *CHRISTIAN ENGSTRÖM,*
*MEMBER OF EUROPEAN PARLIAMENT*

Over and above this, drawing from experience, if designing an activist swarm today, I would have four *function leaders* at every geography in addition to the overall leaders: one function leader each for PR/media, for activism, for swarmcare, and for web, information, and infrastructure. (These are roughly in order from most extroverted to most introverted.) All of these could — and maybe should — have their deputy in turn.

 The typical support functions needed are PR/media, activism, swarmcare, and web.

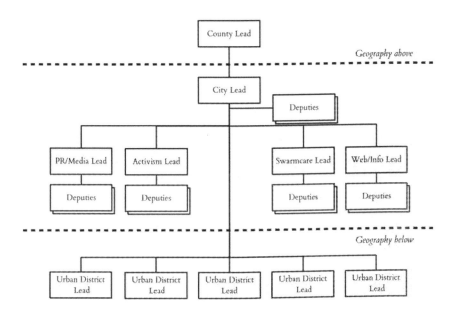

The person responsible for *PR/media* would be responsible for interactions with oldmedia (newspapers, television, radio, etc.) at his or her particular geography. That includes sending press releases, making sure press kits with information are available, and other things related to serving oldmedia with information about the swarm and its activities. (We'll be returning to exactly what this is in chapter 9.)

The *activism leader* would not lead activism as such, but rather support it (as is the case with all of these roles). Whenever activists decide swarmwise that they want to stage a rally, hand out flyers, put up posters, or do some other form of visible activism, this is the person responsible for the practical details, such as PA equipment, permits, and other details on the ground to make things happen.

The person responsible for *swarmcare* would welcome new activists into the swarm and continually measure the overall health of it. A typical task would be to call new activists just to make them feel welcome, and tell them when the next events — social as well as operational — take place. This is more than enough for one person to chew.

Finally, the *information-and-web* guy is the person who maintains the infrastructure of a blog or other web page that summarizes the relevant information of the swarm in this particular geography. (This person also communicates internally when events, such as rallies, happen. The swarm decides when and if they happen; it is the job of this person to communicate the consensus.)

Of course, your needs may vary. Consider this a template that you can use as a starting point. In any case, these boxes are all empty to begin with; organic growth is crucial.

People should not be appointed to these positions just because it's fun to have a title; rather, the organizational chart should lag slightly behind the observed reality. When somebody has already taken on the de-facto role of fixing all the practical stuff for rallies, for example, and everybody already knows that that person is the one to call to get the PA to a rally — that's when the org chart should be updated to reflect that. The person who should update the formal roles is the geography leader, who is responsible for keeping the swarm at optimal conditions in this particular geography.

One person should have one role in the scaffolding, with any kind of multirole person being a temporary measure. In this, watch out for people who start advertising many titles in their signature or similar places — that's a sign they're more after the titles themselves than a single responsibility to do well.

Empty boxes in the scaffolding's organization chart are not bad. They can and will fill up as time passes and groups fill up to the magic size limits and need to break out into subswarms. Don't unnecessarily appoint people to roles because you think empty boxes look bad: an occupied box will block somebody else from filling that role, and so may be preventing the overall growth of the swarm if the person originally appointed to the box wasn't really interested.

Do not be afraid of empty boxes in the org chart.

So do not be afraid of empty boxes in the organizational chart. They provide opportunity for somebody to step up to the plate informally, at which point the chart can be updated to reflect reality. It can help to think of the organizational chart as the map rather than the terrain — when there's a conflict between the two, the terrain wins every time. The organizational chart is an estimate, at best, of what the organization actually looks like.

(This does not apply to military maps. When those have misprints, the military modifies the terrain to match the printed map, which happened at least once during my army term.)

## MEETINGS AS HEARTBEATS

In a typical office setting, people keep in touch about day-to-day operations in quite natural ways — by bumping into each other in the corridor, over coffee, but also in formal meetings. When working with a swarm, almost all of the cooperation happens over a distance — so you must find ways to compensate for the lack of eye contact and subtle body language that otherwise keep a team jelled.

One of the easiest ways to do this is to have regular meetings over the phone or over a chat line where you just synchronize what's going on and where people are with their respective work items (*volunteered* work items) to make that happen. The purpose isn't for you to check up on what's going on — the purpose is for everybody to know the state of the whole.

These meetings should be limited to seven people if on the phone, or thirty people if in a chat channel. Otherwise, they can quickly turn into noise. You should have such regular heartbeat meetings once a week or once every other week with the people closest to you in the swarm's scaffolding, and those people in turn should ideally have heartbeat meetings with their nearest crew as well.

Some swarms or subswarms have preferred physical meetings. While such meetings provide for a lot higher bandwidth and opportunities to sync up, prevent conflicts, and brainstorm ideas, their timing and location can also serve to lock out activists from engaging in the swarm — often inadvertently. For example, if you have a subswarm in a city that meets every Sunday afternoon, you can get lots of students engaged in the swarm — but the choice of Sunday afternoons will make sure that no working parents will ever show up to the meeting, as this is prime family time. Such factors need to be considered, and it is easy to be blind to limitations outside of your own demographic that prevent people in a certain stage of life from attending.

Once method I used to make it easier for people to attend the party management meetings when I was party leader was to limit the meeting to a strict time frame. We would start the meeting at 8 p.m. on Tuesdays, and the meeting would end at 9 p.m., no matter whether everybody thought we were finished or not. That made sure that two things happened: it let people know that they could plan things with their family after 9 p.m. on Tuesday evenings, and it forced people to address the important things first, as the meeting cutoff would happen whether they were done or not.

In short, the simple rule of having a hard meeting cutoff time made sure that people (including me) didn't waste other people's time.


## MEETINGS GONE OVERBOARD

Speaking of wasting other people's time, some activists will tend to take meetings a little too seriously. It is important that you maintain meetings as a necessary evil, because people who are eager to be part of the swarm can easily see meetings as *the purpose of the swarm* — they will tend to see meetings as *work itself*, rather than the short time frame where you report and synchronize the actual work that you do between the meetings.

Bureaucracy and administration will very easily swell to become self-justifying, even in a swarm of activists. Do not let this happen. Keep reminding people that meetings are there for the purpose of synchronizing the work done to advance the external purpose of the swarm, and that every minute spent with each other is a minute not spent changing the world.

> "THE BUREAUCRACY IS EXPANDING TO MEET THE NEEDS OF THE EXPANDING BUREAUCRACY."
> — OSCAR WILDE

In particular, activists in a subswarm dealing with oldmedia (newspapers, television, etc.) can easily become self-absorbed in their own titles: "I attend the media meetings, therefore, I work with media, and thus, I am *really cool*." We'll return to that particular problem in chapter 9.

## A CULTURE OF LEADERSHIP AND TRUST

As the swarm's founder, you must be aware of the human psychology of leadership. People will do as you do, *exactly* as you do, even if and when you are having one of the worst days of your life.

If you show yourself in a thoroughly wretched mood to a swarm of fifty thousand people, they will all emulate your behavior from that day, down to the most minute of details. This is not what you want.

So, ironically, one of the most important parts in founding and leading a swarm is to take good care of yourself. Sleep well, eat well, work out, allow yourself time and space to breathe. This is for the good of the swarm, and has the nice side effect of being good for you, too. If you feel aggressive, short-tempered, and frustrated one day, you should probably refrain from all interactions with the swarm until that passes; if you don't, those moods will become core organizational values.

 If you're not taking care of yourself, you're not taking care of your swarm.

On the flip side of that coin, understanding, patience, collegiality, and passion are values that you want to show. Be aware of your own mood, and know that the swarm copies you — whether you are behaving in ways that set the swarm up for long-term success or catastrophic infighting, the swarm copies your behavior in more detail than you can notice consciously.

One value that you must absolutely communicate for the swarm to work is *trust*. You need to trust in people in the swarm to further the swarm's goals, even if they choose a different way of doing so than you would have chosen, and even if you can't see how it could possibly work.

You also need to communicate that everybody must trust each other in this regard. Leading by doing is necessary here, but not sufficient; you need to periodically repeat that one of the core values of the swarm is that we trust each other to work for the swarm in the ways that we can do so as individuals.

It turns out that one thing that makes swarms so outstanding in efficiency is their *diversity*. People come from all walks of life, and once they realize they have a full mandate to work for the swarm in the ways that they can, they will just do so.

In the Swedish Pirate Party, we had manifested this through a *three-pirate rule*, which can easily be translated into a three-activist rule for any swarm. It went like this: if three activists agree that something is good for the organization, they have a green light to act in the organization's name. It's not that they don't need to ask permission — it goes deeper than that. Rather, they should never ask permission if three activists agree that something is good.

Asking permission, after all, is asking somebody else to take responsibility for your actions – no, take *accountability* for your actions. But a swarm doesn't work like that. Also, the person who would have given that permission would probably be in a worse situation to determine if this action would work in the context the original activists had in mind.

 Asking permission is asking somebody else to take accountability for your actions.

Of course, many balk at this. Letting activists run loose like this? Trusting them with your name and resources to this extent? I heard frequently that it would be a recipe for disaster.

In the five years I led the Swedish Pirate Party, peaking at fifty thousand members during that time, this was not abused once. Not once.

It turns out that when you look people in the eyes and say, "I trust you," and give them the keys to the castle, many are so overwhelmed by the trust that they don't hesitate a second to accept that mantle of responsibility.

It's also important that this was only a mechanism for self-empowerment, and never a mechanism that allowed three activists to tell somebody else what to do or not do.

As a final note on trust, the part about trusting people to act for the best interest of the swarm is crucial. This means that there is never a blame game; if something goes wrong, the swarm deals with it after the fact and never spends time worrying in advance about what might go wrong.

If something doesn't go as intended, the swarm learns from it and moves on. On the other hand, if something is wildly successful, it gets copied and remixed across the swarm with new variants to get even better. This happens organically, without you needing to interfere, as long as activists can publish their successes.

In the next chapter, we'll take a closer look at how activists of the swarm interact with the outside world, learn from mistakes, and remix the successes to evolve and improve.

*May 31, 2006, at about 1:15 p.m.*

*With my brutal but effective interviewing methods being a scary mix of famous and infamous, I have been doing contract headhunting for an executive position all morning, and I am on the last leg on my way home when my cell phone rings. The display says "Peter Piratebay" and shows Peter's famous face. I hit the green "take call" button.*

*"Hey, Peter, good to hear from you, what's up?" We exchange pleas-antries for maybe two minutes, until he interrupts the pleasant tone with "Something has happened that you should probably know about. The police raided the Pirate Bay this morning."*

*I realize immediately that this requires me to mobilize every branch, twig, and leaf of the organization. As I arrive back at the office in my home, I immediately send red-alert texts to the phones of all officers and volun-teers in the Pirate Party, and tell the people in the general chat, "We need a press release on this. It needs to be out within an hour."*

*About an hour later, amid people calling me frantically to check if the text is true, we get the press release out. At that point, television stations start calling me for the first time. In a few hours, we follow up with another press release with the facts we have learned in the meantime.*

*The raid had been a violation of rights on pretty much every conceivable level, which the establishment just ran over like a steamroller. When the system was threatened, rights, shmights.*

*That night, I do my first TV news appearance, and I get on the morning news the next day, too. In the following week, my face is on television every hour on the hour across pretty much all channels. The Pirate Party triples its member base. People are outraged.*

*In fury, people decide to overload the police web servers, making them unreachable. Online newspapers hold polls on whether people think the police or the Pirate Bay will come back online first. The Pirate Bay wins the poll by a landslide.*

*Three days after the raid, on June 3, I give my first widely acclaimed speech, "Nothing New Under the Sun," in a protest rally at the same time as the Pirate Bay comes back online. At the rally, people highlight how the government is way behind technologically, holding banners saying "Give us back our servers, or we'll take your fax machine."*

# CHAPTER FOUR

# Control the Vision,
# but Never the Message

**People's friends are better marketers toward those people than you, for the simple reason that they are those people's friends, and you are not.**

In the last chapter, we talked a lot about formal structures of the swarm. We talked about keeping the working groups to seven people in size, and about splitting the informal groups that approach 150 people in size into two groups. This kind of advice will have come as a surprise to some, who would believe and maybe even insist that a swarm must be leaderless and fully organic.

I do not believe in leaderless organizations. We can observe around us that change happens whenever people are allowed to inspire each other to greatness. This is leadership. This is even leadership by its very definition.

In contrast, if you have a large assembly of people who are forced to agree on every movement before doing anything, including the mechanism for what constitutes such agreement, then you rarely achieve anything at all.

Therefore, as you build a swarm, it is imperative that everybody is empowered to act in the swarm just on the basis of what he or she believes will further its goals — but no one is allowed to empower himself or herself to restrict others, neither on his or her own nor through superior numbers.

This concept — that people are allowed, encouraged, and expected to assume speaking and acting power for themselves in the swarm's name, but never the kind of power that limits others' right to do the same thing — is a hard thing to grasp for many. We have been so consistently conditioned to regard power as power, regardless whether it is over our own actions or over those of others, that this crucial distinction must be actively explained: there is a difference between the ability to empower yourself to perform an action and the ability to restrict others from performing that action. In the swarm, people have the former ability, but not the latter. We will return to explore this mechanism in more detail in chapter 6, as we discuss how to create a sense of inclusion and lack of fear as we shape the general motivations and internal culture of the swarm.

As a result of this far-reaching mandate, somebody who believes the swarm should take a certain action to further its goals need only start doing it. If others agree that the action is beneficial, then they will join in on that course of action.

The key reasons the swarm should not be leaderless are two. You will notice that I refer to "its goals." Those come from you, the swarm's founder. If the swarm were allowed to start discussing its purpose in life, then it would immediately lose its power to attract new people — who, after all, feel attracted to the swarm in order to accomplish a specific goal, and not out of some general kind of sense of social cohesion. If the goal is vague or even under discussion, the swarm will not attract people — because they wouldn't see the swarm as a credible or effective vehicle for realizing their goal. After all, the goal of the swarm is uncertain and unclear if it is under discussion, so what goal would we be talking about in the first place?

The second reason the swarm should not be leaderless is these very mechanisms, the swarm's culture of allowing people to act. These values will be key to the swarm's success, and those values are set and established by you as its founder. If the swarm starts discussing its methods of conflict resolution, putting the swarm in a state where there is no longer any means to even agree whether people have arrived at an agreement, then the necessary activism for the end goal will screech to a halt.

Therefore, I believe that leaderless swarms are not capable of delivering a tangible change in the world at the end of the day. The scaffolding, the culture, and the goals of the swarm need to emanate from a founder. In a corporate setting, we would call this "mission and values."

That said, I also believe in competition between many overlapping swarms, so that activists can float in and out of organizations, networks, and swarms that best match the change they want to see in the world. One swarm fighting for a goal does not preclude more swarms doing the same, but perhaps with a slightly different set of parameters from a different founder. This is fundamentally good for the end cause.

So the sum of this little introspective reflection at the start of the chapter is that the vision of the swarm's end goal comes, and must come, from you — its founder. However, as we shall see, this doesn't mean that you can control the message being told to every single being, or that you should even try to do so. Rather, you should encourage the opposite.

## YOU DO THE VISION, THE SWARM DOES THE TALKING

Traditional marketing says that a message needs to stay constant to penetrate. My experience says that's not very effective when compared to swarm techniques.

It may certainly be true that you can influence routine buying patterns or even routine voting patterns with simpleton messages of the one-size-fits-all type. But if you want energized activists, people who walk an extra mile to make a difference, then it's a different ballgame entirely.

You don't want a routine pattern when you're looking for activists. You want people who are passionate, who feel like kings or queens of the world, and who can't wait to make a difference with their bare hands.

Try to do that with centrally designed TV ads. You can't. No matter how many millions you spend on an ad, it cannot be done. (This disregards the fact that swarms form in cash-strapped environments in the first place.)

> "A MAN DOES NOT HAVE HIMSELF KILLED FOR A HALF-PENCE A DAY OR FOR A PETTY DISTINCTION. YOU MUST SPEAK TO THE SOUL IN ORDER TO ELECTRIFY HIM."
>
> — *NAPOLEON BONAPARTE*

Our language is a social marker. Our choice of words matters, as do minute details in their pronunciation and timing. Our language is a marker of group inclusion, and, more importantly, of group exclusion.

If somebody comes up to you and tells you a factual statement in a language that you identify as that of a group you dislike, you are very likely to discard that message as false, no matter whether it's true or not when analyzed rationally. In the same vein, if somebody that dresses, speaks, and acts in a manner consistent with your social standards tells you a factual statement, then you are likely to accept it as plausible and maybe examine it on its own merits later.

The recipe is ridiculously straightforward: communicate your vision to everybody, and let the thousands of activists translate your vision into words that fit their specific social context. Don't make a one-size-fits-all message that everybody has to learn. It will be one-size-fits-none.

This sounds obvious in hindsight. It has been used in some legacy product marketing, like that of Tupperware's plastic containers, but never on an Internet scale and time. Some political campaigns try to tailor their messages to demographics, but have to abide by general demographic guesses rather than actual social presence.

Let me give a tangible example. When I speak about the opportunities associated with the obsolescence of the copyright industry, I can do so in many different languages. If I were to speak about this before a liberal entrepreneur crowd, I would say something like this:

*"There is tremendous opportunity in the cutting of this link from the value chain. The copyright industry intermediaries no longer add value to the end product or service, and so, in a functioning market, they are going to die by themselves. There is a problem here, as their statutory monopoly prevents that. Therefore, we must assist in this cutoff, as removal of their overhead allows for growth of the overall market, future opportunities for the artist entrepreneurs, and for new jobs that take the place of the obsolete ones."*

However, speaking to dark-red communist groups that celebrate the Red Army Faction as heroes, I would choose a different language:

*"I think it is glorious that the cultural workers have finally assumed control over their means of production, and that we finally have the ability to throw off the middlemen parasite capitalists who have been profiting for decades off of the workers' hard labor. We should help our brothers and sisters to make this transition happen, and help them turn the captured middlemen profits into new jobs for our culture."*

Factually, these two statements are completely identical. I am saying *the exact same thing*. But one wording would not work for the other group; you would get thrown out of the room, and any curiosity about your swarm would be discarded for good.

Granted, these two settings are extreme contrasts to make a point. But even a subtle sign of not belonging can be enough to get your idea and vision discarded in a conversation.

This is why you need the activists — thousands of them — to translate your vision into as many different social contexts as you have activists. Only then will you be able to electrify their friends with your vision, as that vision is clad in the language of their respective social contexts.

Don't think you can do this yourself for every setting. You can't master every nuance of language and social code. Nobody can. I may be able to switch languages rudimentarily from years of training in different settings, but I can't easily change appearance. If I arrive in a suit at a location where I am to give a presentation, and the people there turn out to be laid-back hippie types, then that's it. No word I say after that can change their perception of me.

It is also important, and imperative, that your activists not only are encouraged to translate your vision, but also to *interpret and apply it* to specific scenarios. In a political swarm, for example, that means they need to be able to translate general principles into specific policy on the fly, and express it in appropriate language for the context — always without asking permission. The previously mentioned three-activist rule can apply here, or you can empower everybody individually straight off the bat. When this starts to happen without any central planning and control, the swarm starts to really fly.

There will be people in the swarm who object to others' interpretations of the vision and general principles, of course. This brings us back to the distinction between empowerment of the activist self versus the power to crack down on the work of others. The golden rule of the net springs to life: *"If you see something you don't like, contribute with something you do like."*

This rule is absolutely paramount, and it is you who must enforce it.

Enforce the principle of "If you see something you don't like, contribute with something you do like."

One of the worst things that can happen to the swarm is the emergence of a backseat driver culture, where those who take initiatives and risks are punished for it — and it is your responsibility to make sure that people who do things are rewarded, even when you think they weren't exactly on the money. It is especially crucial that peers in the swarm don't fear other people being angry with the swarm, and punish the risk-taker as a result. After all, people getting angry with you is a symptom that you're starting to cause change, that you're starting to succeed in your mission. This is expected and should not be feared.

This is so important — the swarm lives or dies with this — that it deserves repetition:

When people in the swarm get criticized by the public and by influential people, that is a sign you're on the right track. This is not something to fear, this is something to celebrate, and everybody in the swarm must know this. People must be rewarded by their peers for taking risks, and you must make sure that other people in the swarm reward other people for taking risks, even when things go bad (or just don't produce the expected results). If people see something they don't like, the rule must be that their response is to contribute themselves with something they do like.

In contrast, if, out of fear for being criticized by the public, people start cracking down on one another when they take initiatives, a backseat driver culture will emerge that punishes the activists who take risks and do things they believe in. If a backseat driver culture emerges, risk taking and initiatives don't happen, because activists become shell-shocked from constant peer criticism whenever they try something. If this pattern develops, *the swarm dies.*

You need to celebrate every time somebody does something you feel goes in the right direction and that initiative is criticized by somebody influential outside the swarm. "Well done," you need to say visibly. "These influential people say we're morons. You're doing something right." Lead by example and teach others to celebrate when this happens.

We'll talk more about that in chapter 9: if you're not making anybody outside the swarm angry at all, you're probably doing things the wrong way, and before people outside the swarm get angry, they will always try ridiculing those activists in the swarm who threaten their influence. If somebody says you're all morons and clowns, that's a sign you're on the right track. If they get angry with you, that's even better.

This doesn't mean you can't listen to feedback and learn from it. But it should never, ever, be feared. This is paramount.

## HELP THE SWARM REMIX THE MESSAGE

The previous chapter discussed the vertical communication in the swarm. The horizontal communication is even more important to the swarm's success.

Activists must have the ability to inspire and learn from one another without you as a bottleneck in between them. They need to be in control of the message, as translated from your vision.

What you need to provide for the swarm is some kind of work area where the activists can share work files with one another: posters, flyers, blog layouts, catchy slogans, campaign themes, anything related to spreading your ideas and vision. Also, they must have the ability to comment on and discuss these work files between them.

When you do, you will be amazed at the sheer brilliance many will show in translating your vision into words and images. Not all the posters and flyers will be great, of course, but those that are will be used in a lot more places and situations than the one they were originally made for. All without you interfering.

What's more, the swarm will remix its own posters and flyers all by itself — it will keep evolving them into something better. Some attempts will fall flat on their face. Those that the swarm recognizes as great will live on and be used in new situations, and be remixed yet again.

The ability for the swarm to work horizontally like this, across all boundaries and all scales, is crucial for success. Speaking of flyers and posters, by the way, we arrive at the next vital part:

## TAKE TO THE STREETS

Going back to the social mechanisms of accepting ideas, it is not really enough that people hear the swarm's message from their friends, in particular their friends and acquaintances online.

We come back to the importance of inclusion and exclusion, and how vital it is for people to meet somebody they can identify with who carries the ideas visibly. Group psychology is everything here. When this happens, the ideas can carry over to the new individual.

The keys here are two: "meet" and "identify with." People need to see the swarm in the streets on their way to work or school, and in random places in their daily life. They need to understand that this is something that takes place online and offline, in other places than just in their circle of friends.

This is not as impossible as it may sound.

Let's take a look at how a competing political party experienced the events leading up to the success of the Swedish Pirate Party in the European elections of 2009:

*"Our election workers all paint the same image: the Pirate Party was on practically every square in the entire country, talking to passersby, handing out flyers, and flying their bright colors." — election analysis from the Social Democrats, 2009*

Now, knowing the actual level of activity in the European election campaign that the above quote refers to, I know that "on practically every square" is a stark exaggeration of the actual events that took place. However, the above quote is the subjective impression of reality from a competing political party who had tons of resources and people everywhere. Therefore, it is not far-fetched to say that this represents the actual public impression.

Thus, you should know that it is perfectly possible to give the above impression without any resources, money, or fame — just using swarm techniques.

We'll return to leadership styles that help accomplish this in the next chapter. For now, it's enough to note that there are four classical ways to take to the streets — handing out flyers, putting up posters, having tables or similar in squares, and staging rallies.

Each of these carries its own techniques and experiences. Let's look at them one by one.

Most people who hand out flyers have little or no training in doing so. You'll all too often see people tasked with handing out flyers for various causes, but who look just lost, standing on their own in a corner of the street, huddling in the shadows, holding out a piece of paper to passersby who have no interest in their existence whatsoever. This is a waste of money, brains, and time. Over six years, we have learned a couple of simple techniques that make flyer handouts work in practice. It is your duty to teach this initially, and teach others to teach it in turn. (Of course, you need not follow this experience to the letter. Copy and remix to your needs and desires.) This technique takes about five minutes to demonstrate ahead of every flyer handout activity, and *should* be demonstrated ahead of every flyer handout.

Let's start with the flyer design. It needs to look professional, but need not be perfect nor packed with information: the key thing when handing out flyers is that people see the swarm's symbol and colors and an easily absorbable message, with a link where they can get more information.

In the same vein, the people handing out flyers should be wearing clean and nice-looking clothes with the swarm's symbol and colors. Polo shirts are better than T-shirts here. For the same reason, in cold climates, handing out flyers in summer and spring is much preferable to doing so in winter.

Ideally, a handout lasts about ninety minutes over a weekday lunch, or over a couple of hours shopping midday on Saturday or Sunday, and has about ten people participating.

The people handing out flyers walk slowly in patrols of two, side by side, some three to five meters (ten to twenty feet) apart, up and down a designated part of a street or mall. Three to five meters is close enough to look organized to people they meet, but not close enough to cause individuals on the street to feel threatened in a two-against-one situation. Nobody hands out flyers alone, ever: this will look like an "end of the world, end of the world, end of the world, somebody please take my flyer and read about the end of the world" village idiot who people will want to just cross the street to avoid.

The individual hander-out uses three phrases in a specific order when he or she meets people walking slowly down the street or mall: "Hello" to get eye contact; "Here you are, sir/ma'am" with a smile as he or she hands over a folder or flyer faced so the person may read it at a glance before deciding whether to take it or not; and then "thank you" whether they take it or not. This is simple, effective, and works in all parts of Sweden.

(Perceptions vary somewhat. In the slower-paced northern parts of the country, like Lapland, people may think you're a bit impolite for not at least staying for coffee after having addressed them. In the higher-paced capital of Stockholm, people may think you're a bit impolite for addressing them at all. But the technique *works*.)

If they don't accept the flyer, the hander-out puts it at the bottom of the stack and offers a fresh flyer to the next person. Nobody will accept a flyer that he or she saw being rejected by the person right in front of him or her.

Ideally, the handers-out carry two stacks of items to hand out: one flyer, which is the main event of the day, and one folder with more information about the swarm to give to people who ask for more information. Some will.

One person needs to stay with the stockpile of flyers and other equipment so that handers-out can refill their stacks periodically. Another person needs to organize the event and be formally responsible in case there's trouble, someone whom the handers-out can point at to deal with any complaints. This person also designates the locations of the patrols of two people each in a pattern which causes most people who are out that day to pass at least two patrols: somebody who sees the same flyers being handed out by two different groups of people will get a positive impression of a well-organized activity.

It is quite common for people accepting flyers to start asking questions to the activists handing them out. In this case, make sure that the activists are comfortable responding to the most common questions about the swarm. Having that folder with more information as a backup for the flyer helps in this scenario, too.

As for planning of print runs, a general guideline is that just over a thousand flyers per hour are handed out when working in a group like this.

Finally, some people will inevitably crumple up the flyer or tear it to pieces and throw it with contempt in the street. Make sure that everybody in the activity picks up such litter and throws it in proper trash cans — otherwise, people will register the swarm's colors and symbol as trash in the street, and associate negatively from there.

Putting up posters is somewhat less elaborate, but needs to be done with respect for the person who will be tearing down the posters. Never superglue posters to façades unless your swarm needs to be associated with vandalism, for instance.

In general, our experience says that posters should be put up by patrols of three activists. The first activist holds the poster to the wall, the second affixes it there using masking tape, and the third explains what the poster and the swarm is about to the passersby who will invariably stop in curiosity.

A good guideline is that a one-hundred-poster campaign is a large and quite visible campaign for a suburb or the center of a small city, but it will not last for long: a few days at the most, maybe just a few hours. So choose the timing well. It is better to have rotating teams in a town putting up one hundred posters between them once a week, rather than spending a whole day putting up five hundred posters once that are all gone the next day.

When it comes to hosting book tables or other semifixed installations in streets or open-air trade shows, it is less of a science. Have plenty of materials to give out, make sure that there are always people to man the station, and have the swarm's symbol and colors flying everywhere. You will probably not be able to afford umbrellas and similar elaborate merchandise at this stage, but a couple of flags for display come cheaply at print-on-demand stores.

A tip is to hand out helium-filled balloons with the swarm's colors and symbol to parents who pass by with kids. The kids love it, the parents will tie the balloon to the stroller, and they become a walking billboard for your swarm. People on all sides of your table will start noticing balloons several hundred meters away. (Teenagers, on the other hand, love the balloons for running around the corner with them to inhale the helium, laugh at their funny voices for a breath or two, then come running back for more. There's a fine line in choosing who to give balloons to.)

Finally, rallies and street protests. Arrange a speaker list with six to ten speakers, and make sure that the rally as a whole doesn't last longer than an hour. Police permits may be required for PA equipment (and you do need that). You may be able to gain a wider audience by inviting speakers from neighboring swarms or other organizations sympathetic to your cause.

Your choice of venue matters. You want to fill a square with people to make effective media imagery. If you pick a large square and get 500 people to attend, they will look like a speck in the middle of an empty square. In contrast, in a small square, that same crowd will look almost like an angry, unstoppable mob. It is hard to estimate how many will attend your swarm's rally before even having announced it, but you must do so before choosing where to hold it.

Rallies can be very effective when people are really angry about something that has just happened, compared to staging rallies as a "just because" activity. When people are angry, they will tend to want to share, show, and vent that in groups. This also gives the speakers at the rally a relatively easy task; they basically just have to describe how angry they are at what has just happened, in the most colorful and provocative of terms, to draw thunderous applause at the rally.

This requires quick reactions and turnarounds. A rally the day after or the weekend after an unjust high-profile verdict could be a very effective example. As verdicts are generally predictable in time (but not in content), you and the swarm are able to plan for the possibility of needing such a rally and get the necessary police permits weeks in advance. You may not use those plans, but they should be ready at hand.

When you've made the go decision for a rally, make sure that the media know about the rally in advance (send press releases the previous day or the day before) and put the speakers you want to be seen in media as faces for your swarm in the first and second speaker slots. Media will arrive at the rally, get their pictures and footage, and leave; they do not stay for the full duration.

Make sure to get your own footage and photos from the rally as well. Later down the road, TV stations and newspapers will ask you for cutaway footage and activity images to go with their stories about you. If you can't provide that, they will make a story about somebody else, so this is quite important. For video footage, use a tripod and an HD camera. You can't get broadcast-quality images when using a camera handheld. If you don't have somebody with professional experience in filming, don't try to get moving and panning scenes; it takes a lot of experience to get such scenes usable for broadcast. Instead, just get good footage showing a large crowd from several angles, footage where the camera doesn't move in the scene itself.

As the rally disperses, do close with telling the people of a gathering spot afterward for those who want to get to know one another and just hang out. This helps reinforce friendships in the swarm, and therefore the organization as a whole. Also, new activists are frequently recruited when this happens. In summertime, you may want to bring blankets, picnic baskets with bread, cheese, salami, grapes, and such, and a couple of bottles of wine, to head for a grass spot in a nearby park. That makes for a very friendly hangout after the rally.

Again, in cold climates, avoid rallies in winter altogether. Odds are you'll just get a couple of dozen huddling, freezing people that look terrible on the evening news. (There are exceptions. Don't count on being one of them.)

In any case, limit any winter rally to about thirty minutes.

## SCALE OUT, OUT, OUT

A key concept of the swarm is "scaling out." This refers to the process of moving every activity as far out toward the edges of the swarm as possible, involving as many people as possible — and, while we're doing so, scaling out the swarm's operating costs along with the activity.

Scaling out is an IT term. When something grows in size, in the language of the IT industry, you can scale up or out your server park. Scaling *up* means that you replace the servers currently doing the work with more expensive servers. Scaling *out* means that you keep the low-cost servers currently doing the job, and add more such low-cost servers. We're adding more activists. Many more activists. We're scaling out our work.

If all operating costs of the swarm were to be paid centrally, they might come together to a substantial sum. If done by an activist at the edge of the swarm, just covering his or her portion of the activity, the cost might be so small that the activist may not even think of it in terms of a cost. This is a positively huge benefit of scaling out.

One example could be the flyers we just discussed. If you have an activist swarm with reasonable geographical coverage on the ground, and were to distribute flyers to households, the traditional way of doing so would be to purchase the printing and mailing of the flyers. But with a swarm, you don't need to do that.

Rather, think in terms of making an A5-size or half-letter-size PDF for the flyer and asking your activists to print two hundred copies each and distribute them to their neighbors. It's not only OK to do so, it's even quite expected. Sure, you might not get 100 percent coverage on the ground compared to paying for printing and distribution, but let's do the math here, just for fun.

Assume we have ten thousand activists and that 5 percent of them take us up on this particular request, which is a fair guesstimate for such a request. That means we get one hundred thousand flyers distributed to households near where our current activists live (also suggesting that those places are demographically the right locations to recruit more activists to our swarm).

The total cost to you for achieving this reach is three to four hours of work designing the PDF in question and an energizing, encouraging mail to your activists to print and distribute it. The cost is even less if you have good designers in the swarm who like making flyers, or if you're picking one of the existing remixes of your vision in flyer format.

The total cost in a traditional nonswarm organization, on the other hand, is on the order of forty thousand euros to achieve the same result with paying for address lists, printing, packing, and postage — and quite probably with more work hours spent, too, in just the administrative work in placing the necessary orders.

It's not hard to see the very tangible benefits of scaling out.

You can easily apply this principle to printing flyers, too, especially at the early stages of the swarm (the first year or couple of years, before there is a predictable and significant income). Encourage your activists to pick their favorite flavor or flavors of flyer among all the activist remixes of your vision, print some five hundred copies in their printer, and just head out in town and hand them out. All without asking anybody's permission.

Posters are somewhat harder to scale out due to their nonstandard large size, but a surprisingly large number of activists have access to A3-style printing gear somewhere in their daily routines. It doesn't take large print runs when it comes to posters. As already mentioned, a one-hundred-poster campaign is considered a large one in a suburb or small city.

If it goes well, encourage activists to take photos and share when they do activism in the streets. That encourages more people to do the same kind of activism and breeds a friendly competition. We can also use such photos for internal competitions with fun and silly prizes. This helps motivate the swarm as a whole, and also serves to show other people that the swarm is active — potential recruits and adversaries alike.

In the next chapter, we'll take a deeper look at self-organization and making things happen.

*September 2006.*

*One oddity about the Swedish election system is that the ballots don't work like they do in other countries. In most countries, once your party qualifies for elections, your party gets on the one ballot that is used for the election.*

*In contrast, in Sweden, voting works like this: when voting, you go into the polling station and find a number of different ballots lined up, maybe some seventy of them. Each party has its own ballot with the party's name on it, where you can check a candidate name if you like — if you don't, the party's default candidate will be used. When voting, you pick the ballot of the party you intend to vote for plus a number of decoys, accept a voting envelope handed to you by an election official, go behind a screen, insert the ballot of your choice into the envelope and seal it, leave the decoys behind, and come out from the screen and hand your sealed envelope to the election official along with showing your voter card.*

*Here's the kicker: only the incumbent political parties get their ballots distributed to the polling stations, and for free. A challenger party needs to pay for the printing of several million ballots, which is bad enough, but it also needs to distribute them using the hands and feet of its own activists to five thousand polling places on election day morning — everywhere from large stations in Sweden's capital serving thousands of voters each, to remote places in the deepest of the Lapland forests serving less than a hundred voters. Additionally, you need to supply the fifteen hundred advance polling stations with ballots — and keep them supplied, as some of them throw away the challenger parties' unused ballots at the end of the day.*

*In theory, if a challenger party can't distribute its ballots to the polling stations, a persistent voter intending to vote for them can still pick a blank ballot and write in the name by hand. In reality, though, that doesn't happen: if it's not on the menu, it doesn't get picked. If your ballots aren't at the polling stations, they're not being put into voting envelopes.*

*So during the entire month leading up to the election, when all the other parties are in their endgame of campaigning, one of the Swedish Pirate Party's main efforts is setting up the logistics of distributing millions of ballots to activists to make sure that all polling places are and would be supplied, rather than focusing all our efforts on campaigning. Also, a major part of our election budget would go to printing those ballots.*

*You could argue that the game is heavily rigged toward incumbents in this way, and few would protest this observation. Still, as a challenger, you don't have the right to protest the game being rigged against you — you'll just be seen as a whiner who didn't meet the bar.*

*As party leader, it's the thing foremost on my mind. If we don't get the ballots out, all of our work — the opinion building, the flyers, the poster campaigns, the op-eds, the activist work — will have been for nothing. I design a system which lists all of the polling stations, where people can volunteer to man and refill a station close to them. Today, it's not rocket science, but in 2006, this swarmthink was unheard of in politics: central planning was all the rage. We create roles for ballot distribution and manning the polling stations that volunteers can fill themselves. We create functions for putting distribution volunteers on different levels in touch with one another, creating a logistics chain. We create metrics, we rank cities against each other, we do everything we can to encourage volunteers to get the ballots out there on election day morning. Getting geeks to do such a thing between 7 a.m. and 8 a.m. on a Sunday morning requires some really heavy motivation on their part.*

*As election day comes, we manage a 97 percent coverage by voter count. I am extremely happy with that number; I had previously set 75 percent coverage as a realistically achievable metric.*

# PART II

---

## LEADING
## THE
## SWARM

# CHAPTER FIVE

# Keep Everybody's Eyes on Target, and Paint It Red Daily

Anybody who has led guilds or raids in **World of Warcraft** can learn how to lead a swarm. Or, for that matter, most entrepreneurs who have led small-scale teams dependent on trust. In essence, it's the same social and psychological mechanisms.

If I had to pick one skill that was crucial in allowing me to lead the Swedish Pirate Party on its journey from two lines in a chat channel to taking seats in the European Parliament, it would be skills and experience in project management.

This term, *project management*, is somewhat of a misnomer in this context. When we talk about *management*, we talk about appointed positions — Dilbertesque pointy-haired bosses, all too often. But good project management is not so much management as it is leadership. Leadership is not an appointed position, like management; leadership is a state of group psychology.

The first time I was trained in the enormous difference between these two concepts, boss and leader, was in my officer's training in the Swedish Army. (I hold the rank of second lieutenant.) Any dolt with pointy hair can be appointed to become a boss in the organizational chart, but in order to lead, you must *deserve* people's confidence and trust.

An organization works at its best when these two roles coincide in the same person. When they don't, the organization works terribly.

This boils down to a breakdown of the concept of *responsibility*. It consists of two equally important parts — *accountability* for a certain result, and *authority* to make that result happen. Accountability and authority must always follow one another as responsibility is delegated.

All too often, you will hear somebody being asked to "take responsibility" for a development gone bad, but what they're really being asked is to take *accountability* for something without the corresponding authority. Unfortunately, taking accountability without such corresponding authority is the same thing as taking the blame for events that go wrong outside of your control. Only the most forward and simultaneously naïve people accept such accountability, and sadly they are all too often sacrificed as corporate scapegoats by those with more ruthless ambitions.

The reverse, authority without accountability, is equally bad. You can almost hear Stalin's maniacal laughter in the background as Eastern Europe was being enslaved when somebody manages to get authority without the accompanying accountability.

 Accountability and authority must always go hand in hand as they are delegated.

The takeaway here is that authority and accountability must always follow each other in the concept of responsibility. Your swarm's leaders will not have much of either, though, to be honest. They may get responsibility for a small budget as your swarm progresses, matures, and grows, but as we recall, they never get to tell anybody what to do — nobody does.

This is also why, as we discussed in chapter 3, the organizational chart of the swarm's scaffolding should lag slightly behind the observed reality. You don't appoint somebody to lead a function —

you observe that somebody is already leading a function, voluntarily taking accountability for it, and ask politely whether they would mind if that fact were made formal in an announcement together with the corresponding authority (if any).

Along the same lines, the crucial project management skills that helped me lead the Swedish Pirate Party into the European Parliament were not the skills you'd learn in a project management class — things about gates, schedules, budgets, or stakeholders. It was much more the soft skills that come with experience: how to maintain a group's motivation, focus, energy, and commitment to deliver.

Incidentally, these were skills I learned as an entrepreneur and a project manager during the dot-com boom of the late 1990s.

I founded my first company at age sixteen and had my first employee at age eighteen, so there was plenty of time to learn. But the environment in the dot-com era was something truly challenging, as people didn't work for the money.

There was such a shortage of skilled coders, system architects, and designers everywhere you went that people could basically walk into any company and say, "Hello, I would like to work here." The response from the company would be, "Yes, sir/ma'am — what salary would you like?"

In this environment, where people would literally have a new job before lunch if they felt like leaving their current one at the morning meeting, it was obvious that people didn't work for the money. People invested their energy, focus, and commitment into changing the world for the better. Having rent and food taken care of was just a necessity ticked off the everyday checklist.

Thus, the psychology of this era — leading companies and projects during the dot-com boom — matches leading a swarm almost to the letter. In swarms, people don't work for the pay, either (there isn't any, to begin with), but they invest their energy, focus, and commitment to make the world a better place. Therefore, the leadership styles that work well are pretty much identical.

Of course, this also dispels the myth that you can't lead a group of volunteers the way you would lead a company. Leadership is exactly the same in both cases. Leadership is *psychology*, and has very little to do with a paycheck and much more to do with deeply ingrained social wiring in human beings.

When I led the Swedish Pirate Party, I used the exact same skill set I had used as an entrepreneur. And it did take the swarm into the European Parliament, so it's hard to argue with the results.

## PROJECT MANAGEMENT AND SELF-ORGANIZATION

The first time you see self-organization happen, it feels like magic. After having communicated a vision, you can see how the people who listened to you start to self-organize to make your vision happen, without you needing to give directions — or, indeed, interfere.

The trick, then, is how to communicate the vision. If I had to give a quick answer to that question, it would be "with all the passion you can muster, from the depths of your heart, through the fire of your voice and the determination of the depth of your eyes." You need to be positively radiant with your desire to change the world for the better, and, above all, communicate three values:

— We can do this.
— We are going to change the world for the better.
— This is going to be hard work for us, but totally worth it.

You will notice that we're talking about changing the world in "we" form. This is crucial. There is never "I need someone to do X," nor is there ever "You should be doing X." There is just "We all need X to happen." You don't need to point at somebody, or even imply who should do it. Somebody will.

 A subtle but important part of leading a swarm is to always talk in "we" form.

Let's take these three values one at a time.

**We can do this:** Part of what energizes a swarm is the realization that the sheer number of activists can make a real difference in the world, and that the task would seem impossible, utterly unattainable, before you came on stage with this crazy idea. It could be changing worldwide policy on a small but important matter, it could be going to Mars, it could be dropkicking an entire archaic industry out of existence with a new, disruptive product or service, it could be solving world famine, illiteracy, or disease. Shoot for no less than the moon! Once you've run the numbers as we discussed in chapters 1 and 2, and communicated to the swarm that your insane idea is actually achievable, blue sparks of energy will jolt across the swarm with loud, crackling noises. People will look high from the excitement of being a part of this. Feel high, too.

(You can and should push it even further, by the way. After all, we've already been to the moon. Everybody knows that. So shoot for Mars instead! That project would energize people, *electrify* people. In contrast, you'll never get a swarm energized around the idea of making the most professional tax audit.)

Keep saying "This is hard work", "This will change the world", "We can do this."

**We are going to change the world for the better:** Keep repeating your vision of how fantastic the world will look after the swarm has succeeded in its ambitions, and how great it would be for humanity as a whole. (Swarm methodologies only work well when you strive for the greater good. Even if you could get a short-term swarm focus around hate and intolerance, all your values become organizational values. Therefore, a swarm built on distrust would quickly be devoured from within by its own negative feelings, and collapse, splinter, and fragment into irrelevance.) The swarms that are the subject of this book aim to go into the history books based on mutual trust to achieve the impossible. The people who devote themselves to the goal of your swarm do so to get a footprint in history. You should communicate that this is exactly what will happen, once the swarm succeeds. (And indeed, getting to Mars *would* get into the history books, as would eliminating illiteracy.)

**This is going to be hard work:** One key value you must never falter on is your honesty. You must always communicate the situation of the swarm and its place in the world exactly as you perceive it, even if that means telling people that the swarm has problems or isn't gaining momentum. (However, you should always think of at least one way out of a bad situation, and communicate that, too — as in *we can do this.*) The key point here is that people should not think that changing the world for the better is going to be easy or come lightly. You said *totally possible.* You didn't say *easy.*

Once you have communicated this to the swarm, you will start to see people thinking in terms of "how can I help make this happen?" When a couple of thousand activists think like this, magic happens.

Also, it is crucial that you allow the swarm's scaffolding to keep growing organically. Train your closest officers in swarm methodology and techniques, as described in this book or remixed with your own flavors of style, and help them recruit new officers into the empty boxes that their own box connects to. Your swarm will always grow from the inside out — it can only grow on its edges, a concept we will return to in chapter 8.

This is part of the necessary scaling out.

## DRAW THE TIMELINE FOR ALL TO SEE

A key tool in project management is the *timeline*. Between now and success, you will need to set subgoals to be met that are spaced about eight weeks apart. This may seem like a contradiction to self-organization, but it's not: you're telling the swarm the things that need to happen to get from point A to point B. You're not saying who should be doing what and when.

There are many good reasons to do this. The first, of course, is to back up the initial energy with credibility in the swarm's ability to deliver:

— *Let's go to Mars!*
— *Yeah!*
— *Yeah...but, eh, how do you do that, again?*
— *Um...*

Setting subgoals, or *milestones* in project lingo, spaced about two months apart on the timeline communicates a path from now to success that not only helps people believe in the swarm, but also helps people choose to do things that are relevant for the current stage of the project. Each subgoal needs to be credible, relevant, achievable, and clearly contributing to the end success. It will also help jell the swarm into crack working teams that perform magic on shoestring budgets (or, more commonly, no budgets at all).

As a tangible example, the first subgoal of the Swedish Pirate Party was registering the party with the Swedish Election Authority. When the party was founded on January 1, 2006, the deadline for registration was eight weeks out. We needed fifteen hundred signatures from identified citizens with voting rights in the imminent elections. This proved to be a perfect task to jell the geographic subgroups: it was a hurdle to clear, there was a deadline, it was doable, and it contributed in a very graspable way to the end success. We arranged a competition between the thirty initial geographic subgroups, where the winners in total count of signatures, as well as the winners in signature count relative to the size of their geography, both would get an original certificate of registration. A silly prize which we paid a small premium for — getting multiple originals of the certificate — but very, very symbolic and worthwhile when you're building a movement that will change the world.

You will notice that I didn't tell anybody how to collect those signatures. That's where swarmthinking kicked in and everybody started sharing his or her experiences in a giant hivemind hellbent on success, not being the slightest bit afraid of learning by trial and error, as we discussed in the previous chapter. One of our best signature collectors at the end of the day was an activist named Christian Engström, who set the benchmark: it was possible to collect twenty signatures per hour if you were out on the streets in midshopping hours. That particular activist is now a Member of the European Parliament.

The second reason you need subgoals about eight weeks apart on a visible, published timeline is to create a sense of urgency. In general, if something is farther out than eight weeks, we don't care about it at all, it's just an arbitrary goal in the future. Your vision needs to be broken down into parts that are small enough that everybody can always see a closing goal on the near-term horizon.

I could mention many software projects here by name, projects that started out as two-year projects without such subdivision, and which, it was invariably realized, wouldn't make it as the deadline approached. Even though it's water under the bridge, I won't name those projects by name here — mostly out of courtesy but possibly also due to nasty NDAs — but I'll share this wisdom of project management:

— *How does a project get to be a year late?*
— *One day at a time.*

The key to shipping on schedule at the end of a project is to stay on schedule *every day*. This doesn't mean that a failure to adhere to the schedule is a failure of the swarm; rather, you as a project manager should have anticipated possible deviations in both directions from the start and allowed for them in the plan. When making development plans, it is typically prudent to leave 10 percent of the time of every subgoal unallocated for unforeseen events. Only you can know how this translates to your swarm, but the key is to *adjust* the schedule and the plan every day to account for changes in a fluid reality. You can't change the events of the past, but you can replan for the future to accommodate for what has already happened.

 Make all the targets visible and show the progress toward them.

Every day, you need to make sure that everybody in the swarm can check how far the swarm as a whole has progressed toward the nearest subgoal and toward the end goal. Paint the targets bright red on a daily basis for everybody to see; make all the targets visible and show the progress toward them.


## SETTING VISIBLE, ACTIVATING, AND INCLUSIVE GOALS

Have you ever played World of Warcraft (or, for that matter, pretty much any modern game)? One thing that catches people's sense of addiction is that there are always many different paths to choose from for getting a reward of some kind. Looking at World of Warcraft, you can level up (called "dinging" from the sound effect when that happens), you can learn skills, you can explore the map, you can get rich, etc. In Battlefield 3 and similar games, you can get all sorts of achievement awards based on how you play the game. There's always something to strive for that suits your taste.

This phenomenon, that there's always some visible, public reward to strive for, no matter your taste, is key to a successful swarm. A lot of this can be achieved by just measuring a lot of things visibly. Anything that you measure in public, people will strive and self-organize to improve without further interference from you.

Let's take that again, because you probably skimmed it while speed-reading, and it is key to the whole swarm leadership concept:

Anything that you measure in public, people will strive and self-organize to improve.

It's basically that simple, and that complex. The Swedish Pirate Party posts its liquidity, assets, debts, and donation summaries openly (as many political organizations do now, but not a lot did so in 2006). This leads to people wanting to break new donation records.

Same thing with membership numbers, and in particular their growth rate.

Same thing with response times to mail. Exposure events in oldmedia (TV, radio, newspapers). Mentions on blogs and Twitter. And so on.

(Some people refer to this as *gamification*, a term that can come across as unnecessarily derogatory. This is not about producing work of low quality because you somehow goof off and think you're playing games while producing it; rather, it's about finding

ways to engage the reward mechanisms of the brain for doing brilliant work in the same ways that successful video games do.)

 Anything you measure in public will get improved. Make sure it's the right thing.

Three things emerge as important here. First, the conclusion that things that aren't measured don't get handled well, or indeed at all. This is partly true. Some things are fun to do anyway and will get done just because of that — this particularly involves social and cre-ative activities. Routine activities that are the same from day to day require some kind of motivating visible mechanism, or, more effi-ciently, a competitive element.

Let's take mail responses as an example. Responding to mail addressed to the swarm at some public request-for-information address is hardly a very visible task, nor is it a very creative one, and yet it is one of the more important ones. Quick response times with proper and correct responses can make or break your swarm once oldmedia decide to try you out. Therefore, this is something we need to pay attention to.

A very working solution to this dilemma is to use internal competitions with silly prizes. (Tangible rewards should rarely be individual in a swarm — always foster teamwork.) Use divisions by geography or some other arbitrary line to create teams that compete against one another in providing helpful answers quickly.

This is the second observation that emerges. If measuring things gets them done (and indeed, there is no upper limit to how many metrics you can or should track publicly), measuring things in internal competitions gets them done even more. As I already mentioned, this is how we jelled the organization in the Swedish Pirate Party right after its founding when collecting signatures for the party's formal registration. There is a social limit to how many competitions you can have working at a time, which is probably higher than one but lower than five — this is up to you and your swarm to find out.

The third observation is the crucial importance of measuring the *right thing*. There are many horror stories of people who measure the slightly wrong thing, and therefore end up with terrible results.

The takeaway for this third point is that some things can't be measured directly, and so you have to find some other thing that you *can* measure that has an assumed or known *correlation* to the thing you want to actually measure. Take alcohol consumption, for example. You can't measure alcohol consumption in a country directly, but you can measure alcohol *sales*. This was done in Sweden a couple of decades ago, and the authorities responsible for public health rejoiced as alcohol consumption — as it was assumed to be, and published as such — went down steadily, year after year.

Then, somebody in charge discovered that about one-third of what Swedes drink is moonshine vodka, *au naturel* or spiced into schnapps. (A proud handicraft of our people, I might add.) This was never sold in regulated stores, and therefore never measured. Bureaucrats who live for rules and regulations had been making false assumptions — that people cared in the slightest about what the law said in this aspect — and alcohol consumption had actually increased steadily, leading to bad conclusions and bad policy as a result of bad metrics.

In the software business, the examples of this are too numerous. People who are rewarded for finding bugs is a common example of such *Heisenberg metrics*.

(Werner Heisenberg was a physicist pioneering quantum mechanics. Quantum mechanics are mind-boggling, a study in masochism to learn, and fortunately quite beyond the scope of this book. The only relevant part here is that, at the quantum level, you can't measure something without simultaneously changing it. This was not discovered by Heisenberg at all, but phenomena similar to this are named after him anyway as he was a famous quantum physicist who happened to discover something else entirely.)

When somebody is rewarded for finding bugs, then, by definition, you measure when they find bugs and probably make it public, in order to herald the best bug finders as an example to follow. However, the instant you measure this and reward people for it, a portion of the people tasked with finding bugs will split that reward with developers who *introduce* bugs and tell them where to look. Therefore, measuring the state of the swarm can change it completely in the measured aspect, if done wrong.

> "I'M GOING TO CODE ME A NEW MINIVAN THIS AFTERNOON."
>
> —*WALLY, FROM THE "DILBERT" COMIC*

This is a typical example of Heisenberg metrics. There was a similar effect with the site *mp3.com*, which was a pioneer in the music-in-the-cloud business. (They were so much a pioneer, in fact, that the copyright industry sued them out of existence, bought the remnants for scrap value, and closed them down.) They had this experiment in 2001 called *pay-for-play* where an artist would get a piece of the site's revenue, shared between the artists on mp3.com according to how much they were played on the site. Thus, a fixed portion of money was to be distributed to the artists of mp3.com, according to objective metrics of their popularity, as measured by the number of track plays on the site for a particular artist.

*Bzzzzt.* Very bad idea. But thanks for playing.

What happened was utterly predictable — everybody wanted to support their favorite artist financially, and therefore set all computers they could access to play music from that particular artist from the site mp3.com, but with the volume turned off as to not disturb anybody. Some people coded playbots that would repeatedly stream an artist's music to boost artificial numbers that translated into money. Heisenberg metrics.

At the end of the day, the conclusion here is that you not only need to visualize the progress toward the nearest subgoal and the end goal of the swarm, but many other metrics as well that indicate the overall health of the swarm's performance. You should pay particular attention to the fact that as you increase the number of metrics visualized, the tasks that don't get measured at all will get less priority. Some of them may be important.

## DIFFERENT LEADERSHIP STYLES

Group psychology and individual proficiency of tasks mature as they gain experience. In different phases of group cohesion and individual proficiency, you need to lead in different ways.

Let's look first at what it takes to train an individual in a new task. It can be something as everyday as handing out flyers, or it can be doing a live debate on CNN or al-Jazeera in front of several million people. The principles are the same, and people can sweat in anxiety before doing either one for the first time.

In general, I find that a model with four leadership styles works well.

These four leadership styles are quite different, and you need to use all of them when leading a swarm, reading each situation and applying the corresponding style. A frequent comparison of these leadership styles is the progression of the narrative in the movie *Karate Kid* (the original, not the remake), and the combination of these styles and the ability to shift between them has been described as *situational leadership*.

It is a vital part of the leadership role to personally train those who regard you as their leader.

When somebody is entirely unskilled in an art, you need to give direct, specific, and explicit instructions. Hold his or her hand entirely. At this stage, you need to focus on the actions to take and how to do them properly, rather than explaining their purpose in the greater scheme of things.

— *Paint fence. Up, down, up, down. Strong wrist.*
— *Wax on, wax off.*

In a swarm scenario, we observe that direct instructions for donations yield much greater results than vague ones. The more decisions you leave up to the reader when doing a call for donations, the less money you'll get. For example,

— *We are out of flyers. It's a luxury problem, as we are handing out more than we thought possible, but it is still a problem. Help us! Log onto your bank and transfer 25 euros into account 555-1337-31337 right now, exactly just right now!*

will yield a result almost an order of magnitude stronger than this version:

*— We'd appreciate if you'd help us fund our handout materials. Please donate any amount you would like to contribute to account 555-1337-31337 at any time in the near future.*

The difference in results lies in the very specific instructions. Every degree of uncertainty leads to inaction at this stage. If you make people comfortable with acting, and lower the bar as far as you can for people to take action within their comfort zone, then things will happen just as you instruct.

 Vary your leadership style with people's experience of the topic at hand.

Same thing with handing out flyers, as we discussed in the last chapter. You need to make sure that every flyer handout is preceded by a very direct and inclusive instruction detailing every part of handing out, like the instructions described in that chapter. This is direct leadership.

The next stage and type of leadership is applied when people have mastered the basic actions, but are getting frustrated over their lack of context. They don't see the road ahead and don't feel progress. At this stage, you need to drop the direct handholding leadership and *encourage* and *explain* why these actions lead to positive results.

— *You're not teaching me karate! You're just using me to paint your fence and wax your car!*
— *Show me: wax on!*

The third stage comes when somebody is proficient in the skills needed, but still not in his or her comfort zone. He or she has the skills and the ability to deliver, but just doesn't know it yet. This makes for yet a third type of leadership, which basically is *endless encouragement.*

— *I'm never going to be any good at this! (makes a backflip from stand-still)*

Finally, the fourth and final stage is when somebody is self-motivated and self-reliant. At that point, he or she has more or less ascended to be your equal and doesn't require much in the way of maintenance. The only important thing is that you periodically recognize him or her when he or she walks an extra mile. In this scenario, the one thing to keep in mind is that you recognize an extra mile only when it really is an extra mile — nobody in the fourth stage wants to be commended for performing trivial and routine tasks well.

You need to assess every individual you work with here — you need to assess where everyone is on this scale *in his or her specific context*. He or she may be in several different places at once if he or she is working in multiple contexts.

To wrap this up, you also need to pay attention to how groups form and mature. Groups, too, will pass through stages.

When new people first meet in a working environment, you can observe them being very polite and friendly with one another. If somebody appears offended, apologies follow immediately. These are symptoms of a group that cannot yet deliver effectively. Politeness is a sign of an inefficient group that hasn't learned how to work as a team; people are keeping distance.

Over time, as these individuals learn to work together, they also explore where their limits go, and these limits of people's roles will start to collide and flow into one another. This is when they start fighting between themselves over rules and culture in the group. This is a significant step forward from overfriendly politeness and shows that the group is well on its way to becoming a well-functioning team.

Finally, in the third phase, you see nothing of the clearly marked distances that were there at the outset. A functioning team can be observed by everybody seeming to know what to do without anybody spelling it out; the group has learned how to work together.

(If new people are added to the mix, the group temporarily reverts into determining roles, culture, and boundaries.)

You need to be aware of these group phases in group psychology, and, in particular, you need to know that a small amount of conflict is actually a step of progress. A group that remains polite to each other has not learned to work well together.

 People that are polite to each other have not yet learned how to work as a team.

We'll take a closer look at group psychology and the inevitable conflict resolution in the next chapter, as we discuss how to make people feel included and constructive.

*September 17, 2006, at 9:00 p.m. sharp.*

*The election day has worked well. We find a lot of reasons that our real base isn't accurately reflected in the polls, which don't include us — starting with the fact that polling institutes only call landline phones, which our supporters typically don't have, and ending with much less reasonable fabrications. At the end of the day, the polls would turn out to be remarkably correct, but we don't know that yet.*

*We are gathered in a restaurant in the laid-back southern parts of Stockholm for an election night dinner. Some thirty people are present. As the exit polls come up on screen and parties are presented one by one, people are silent, eyes fixed on screen. Each party that gets presented has dropped significantly from the last election — for every party presented, there are more and more percent units missing from the total that need to have gone somewhere else.*

*One camera, from a Finnish reporter, is fixed rolling on me as the results come up one by one.*

*Then, bam. The last party to be presented — the Moderate right-center party - climbs 13 percent units, eating up all of the slack. There is no room for a successful challenger party in the small numbers that are left.*

*All the energy drains from the room in a heartbeat. There is no Pirate Party presented at all in the election results. I realize immediately that leadership is needed, and that it is needed right now.*

*I stand up and address the room. "This is not the end," I promise them. "We know that we are needed, and the alternative to fighting for our rights is accepting that they are stripped away. That is not acceptable and that is not going to happen." Energy does not pick up, but at least it stops dropping. The Finnish reporter turns off his camera. There's no more news happening here tonight.*

*The one loud cheer comes from the mock-up school elections, which are held in seventh to twelfth grades. That election is done partly for fun, partly as an indicator for future trends, and is presented on election night along with the real results. As those numbers come up on screen, the Pirate Party has its own bar in the election results, with 4 percent of the vote. We are clearly stronger in the youth segment than in the population overall, boding well for future growth.*

*As I sit down to finish my now-cold spaghetti carbonara, I feel exhausted.*

*"This burger was delicious", says Christian Engström, who sits across from me.*

*"Sure, pick on me for getting the wrong food, too," I reply with a tired laugh.*

# CHAPTER SIX

# Screw Democracy, We're on a Mission from God

The swarm must have mechanisms for conflict resolution, for decision making, and for reward culture. There are many ways to accomplish this. A traditional voting democracy is one of the worst.

We can easily observe that, in any organization, it happens that one person wants to limit what another person in the organization can do. This creates a *conflict*. In general, there are four ways to resolve this situation.

You can say that no person in the swarm has the right to limit what another can do. This would be the typical swarmthink, at least as far as nonscarce resources are involved. (When it comes to money, in case the swarm has any, decisions need to be made.)

You could also determine that 51 percent of the swarm has the right to exercise power over 49 percent of the swarm, which would be a meeting-and-voting scenario. This is not only counter to swarmthink, but it also creates a culture of fear of losing rather than a culture of empowerment and action.

You could also go with the principle of somebody having the final decision. Ruling over others by decree is not only completely counter to swarmthink, but it doesn't work in the first place, as people are volunteers and, quite frankly, do whatever they want.

Finally, you can say that everybody has the power of veto for decisions. While this creates significant border-setting problems with regard to exactly who constitutes "everybody," it is one of the most inclusive ways to get volunteers on board once that problem has been solved. However, it only works well for smaller subgroups (30 or less people).

Let's take a look at each of these four mechanisms.

First, let's discard ruling by decree as effective. That is not how a swarm works, and it would establish you (or other decision-makers) as a bottleneck for everything the swarm needed to do, disabling the swarm's speed, trust, and scale advantages. It also assumes that the ordered person accepts the decree, which she or he has no reason at all to do, being a volunteer of his or her own free will.

This leads us to the next method of conflict resolution, voting. Internal democracy is often heralded as a praise-be-all because it leads to *legitimacy* in the elected decision makers. This is true for a country, and paramount on that stage: when citizens don't perceive their legislators as legitimate, a situation is created which can get quite messy. Democracy has never been the state constitution of choice because of its ability to bring forward the best and wisest managers of a country, but because it has the best ability to stave off disastrous managers, and because the resulting choice of manager has a perceived legitimacy in an environment where all citizens find themselves subjected to the rules of that country.

But legitimacy in a swarm is quite different from legitimacy in a country. People cannot realistically choose to not be in a country, but people do choose to be part of a swarm or not be part of it. Therefore, legitimacy in the decision making of the swarm comes through the fact that people are volunteers in the first place and choose to be part of the swarm, with all the values that come with it.

Therefore, we are free to focus on the conflict resolution mechanisms that produce the best delivery potential for the swarm as a whole. In order for a swarm to function, people need to be happy about being part of it. There is a need to make everybody feel like a winner for pursuing their individual goals through the swarm, rather than choosing to stand outside it.

Here, we arrive at the important key insight:

*The process of voting creates losers.*

People who become losers are *not happy.*

Happy people are productive, enthusiastic, and good activists. Therefore, we want happy people.

---

 Voting creates losers, and losers are un-happy activists who disengage. Don't vote.

---

When it comes to a traditional internal democracy, which is the dangerously easy way out for any conflict resolution, there are important drawbacks and side effects to be aware of. People who anticipate a voting process prepare themselves for the possibility of losing — so they become motivated by *fear of losing personally,* rather than motivated by the joy of building the swarm that furthers their personal goals.

This distortion of motivation in a voting scenario will cause such activists to behave in a completely different pattern than if they were focused entirely on the end goals of the swarm. It creates a significant shift to defensive stances at the individual level that are harmful to the swarm's ability to function. We'll be returning to why.

So, in effect, there are two good ways to resolve conflicts in a swarm.

The first is organizational, and means that we negate the possibility of one person determining what another can do in the first place. Nobody gets to tell anybody else what to do. This is the norm for a swarm. Some people call it a "do-ocracy."

The second effective method is a consensus-making decision process where everybody can veto the way forward. This method is much more costly, but can (and should) be used in rare and carefully selected scenarios where the number of people concerned is graspable – typically 30 or less. Be careful with establishing consensus decisions as an organizational requirement, though – it would be extremely cheap for an adversary to kill the operational ability of the swarm by putting one person in the group to veto every significant decision.

Once you have clarified to the swarm that these conflict resolution methods are the ones we use, some people will *insist* that internal democracy with voting brings legitimacy to decision making. But there is an important underlying assumption at work here: that the collective makes better decisions than the individual activists. As we have seen, the swarm organization relies on the *exact opposite.*

The values we desire in a swarm are inclusion, diversity, and empowerment. But if we are voting on something, we are *limiting* the minority — not empowering them. We are letting a 51 percent majority decide what a 49 percent minority *cannot* do, things that the 49 percent believe would further the swarm's goals. It is therefore highly demoralizing. Also, we are limiting diversity, as the swarm might *need* that crazy 5 percent of activists to succeed in a very specialized social context that only they understand, in order to create the perfect storm of different social contexts that cooperate toward succeeding with the swarm's end goal. Voting as a concept closes and eliminates this route to success. Finally, a swarm is legitimate only because it lets every individual include himself or herself on *his or her own terms* in order to further the swarm's goals.

Therefore, "democratic legitimacy" is a *contradiction in terms* in a swarm organization. The process of voting actively reduces the legitimacy of decision making and involvement, and should be avoided as much as possible.

Instead, let's look more at the other two methods we just high-lighted.

## MERITOCRACY AND THE LAW OF TWO FEET

People accustomed to voting as a catchall panacea will initially have a hard time adjusting to a swarm meritocracy, as they won't get to determine what others shall do and not do. But this concept — that no person can have a say over any other — is part of the swarm's core values.

In a democratic conflict resolution system, individual influence is achieved by the group waiting for a decision point and then voicing individual opinions at that point in time. In a swarm, there is no waiting and there are no such decision points. Rather, influence is achieved by individual leadership and individual appreciation — if you think something needs to be done, you just do it, without ask-ing anybody. If other people think that your initiative is good, they will join in of their own accord. If not, they go elsewhere. Thus, the person taking an appreciated initiative gains immediate influence, which gives the swarm as a whole a tremendous momentum and learning speed.

This has sometimes been expressed as "the law of two feet": It is every activist's right and responsibility to go where he or she feels he or she can contribute the most and, at the same time, get the most in return as an individual. If there is no such place within this particular swarm, an activist will leave the swarm and go elsewhere.

(Just for the record, the law applies equally to people in wheelchairs, disabled veterans, and people who otherwise don't have two actual feet.)

There is no shame for an activist in leaving an activity where he or she cannot contribute and going elsewhere. Quite to the contrary: it is expected and seen as showing respect for the other participants in the activity, who won't have to keep including somebody who doesn't feel he or she can contribute.

In this way, the swarm will take initiatives all of its own that further the swarm's end goal. Activists will gravitate to where they see that they can contribute. And from the founder's perspective, beautiful things just happen without any need for central control or orders.

## EMPOWERING LIKE CRAZY FOR FUN AND PROFIT

The tricky part can be to establish a meritocracy in an environment where people aren't used to it. Again, this can be established through leadership — using the principle of teaching by example, and allowing others to learn through observation. In a swarm, people will copy the behavior of those with a perceived influence. As the swarm's founder, you have the highest amount of initial such influence.

I solved this by establishing the already-mentioned *three-pirate rule* immediately, which was later set in stone as a core organizational principle in the Swedish Pirate Party. As I explained it then, people didn't need to ask permission, and the concept went beyond that: they were specifically *banned* from doing so. Their own judgment was the best available in the organization for their own social context, and they were required to use that judgment rather than aspiring to hide behind somebody else's greenlighting.

Asking permission, after all, is asking somebody else to take responsibility — no, *accountability* — for your actions. But the person asked is in a worse position to make an informed decision, and so may need to gather data to be comfortable with taking on this account-ability. This creates delays and fosters insecurity in the organization.

 Asking permission is asking somebody else to take accountability for your decision.

The key insight here is that even the largest and most rigorous processes can screw up monumentally, to the point where the rest of the world asks out loud what they were thinking. To take a concrete example, one of Sweden's largest labor unions did a large-scale campaign with the slogan "Work gives you freedom." This was a multimillion-euro project by one of the largest organizations in the country.

Of course, the billboards came back down again and ads went off the air in the blink of an eye as soon as somebody pointed out the slight...lack of propriety...in the labor union using the same slogan as the *Auschwitz* extermination camp had used in World War II.

Another very honorable mention concerns the huge hospital land-lord *Locum*, which is a Latin name meaning "place" or "location". In the Christmas ads of 2001, they decided to advertise big. Their logo looks like this, just having their company name in lowercase:

# locum.

However, for this particular occasion, the company decided to portray themselves as a warm and friendly company, and therefore replaced the small "o" in their logo with a big red heart. Then, they plastered the result in full-color advertisements in the biggest Swedish media. I'll leave it to you to picture what message the altered logo *actually* conveyed in those full-color ads.

While these may be humorous episodes on the surface, at the expense of somebody else's facepalming, there's an important lesson here, too. These are thoroughly bureaucratic organizations with stratospherically high budgets that a swarm can never dream of.

If this kind of rich organization can make such monumental mistakes, then no amount of advance checking can safeguard against making mistakes. Once you realize this, that some percentage of things *will* go wrong no matter how many safeguards and checkpoints you put in place, and that this percentage is *fairly constant* beyond the most basic of sanity checks, then you can go into a comfortable zen mode with regard to trusting and empowering others.

For if it doesn't matter how many safeguards you put in place against PR gaffes, there is no point to bother with such safeguards in the first place. Instead, you can focus on optimizing the swarm for speed, trust, and scalability, and we can communicate to the swarm that mistakes *will* happen, and when they do, we *fix* them, *learn* from them, and *move on.*

My approach for a very basic sanity check was to have three people agree on an idea as good for the swarm. One person can come up with ludicrous ideas, but I've never seen two more people agree on such ideas. This was simple, communicable, and effective, yet enough to retain the full speed and agility of the swarm.

But this attitude has another very positive effect. By communicating clearly that in this swarm, you're not only *allowed* to make mistakes, but *expected* to do so from time to time, you encourage the bold attitude required to change the world. You need not only your own crazy ideas, but the crazy ideas of many others to succeed, and you need to create the climate where they are welcome and rewarded.

## MISTAKES ALLOWED HERE

This part is absolutely paramount to communicate to your officers in the scaffolding supporting the swarm — that mistakes are not only allowed, but expected, and when they happen, we learn from them. (It's a different thing to tolerate somebody making the same mistake over and over, or sabotaging the swarm deliberately, but that's not what we're talking about here.)

When forming a swarm, everybody is venturing into unknown territory. By definition, it's a trial-and-error venture. Everybody is breaking new ground in changing the world in a way that has not been tried before — both on the individual and the organizational level.

Since this has not been tried before, there is no right answer or concrete experience to fall back on. Everything done has, to some extent, never been tried before. Therefore, by necessity, it becomes obvious that a lot of things tried won't work out. However, a small portion of the initiatives tried will work out amazingly well, and the swarm will learn from those and build further on them.

The conclusion here is that you must allow things to be tried. The good stuff won't appear if you don't allow the bad stuff to be tried, too. You only know which is which once they've had a chance to work out.

 You must let the unknown be tried and evaluated to find the good stuff.

But it's not enough to allow things to be tried. We have discussed the importance of optimizing the swarm for speed — as in minimizing the time from somebody's idea to somebody's action. But to truly outrun the competition, you need to minimize the *iteration cycle* — the time from a failure to the next attempt at succeeding. Make it possible to learn and try again, learn again and try again, and so on, and communicate that this is not only allowed, but expected.

Failures are expected, but with every failure comes a learning experience. In almost every organization, a number of failures are a prerequisite for an ultimate success with a particular activity. Make it possible to make those failures in as short a time as possible, minimizing the iteration cycle, and your success will come sooner.

Also, it's not necessary to speak of failures, as most people won't see a failure — they will see something that went reasonably OK, but which can be done even better the next time. That's also the appropriate mind-set for maintaining a positive attitude.

With all this said of a meritocracy or a "do-ocracy," there are some instances where parts of the swarm really may need to work as a cohesive group, rather than as individuals following the law of two feet. Collective decision making is always hard, and, as previously discussed, democracy creates losers. This begs the question; is there a method for collective decision making in a small group that *doesn't* create losers? There is not just one, but several. I have a very powerful experience with one such method.

## THE MAGIC OF THE CONSENSUS CIRCLE

One good mechanism for arriving at a decision in a (defined) group is called a *consensus circle*. Rather than focusing on fear of losing through voting, which will cause people who fear losing to just stall what they think is a bad decision, the consensus circle focuses on including everybody and getting people into a constructive mind-set.

I observed this firsthand as we gathered the simulated parliamentary group of the Swedish Pirate Party for a kickoff in the summer of

2010. (We had simulated who might get elected in a sort of best-guess exercise, and, seeing the enormous diversity of the group, we realized that these people needed to learn to work together *before* getting into parliament, or we might just as well hand out name tags saying "BREAKFAST" on getting elected, as that's the only name the veteran politicians in other parties would care to learn.) In this kickoff, there was a routine issue the group was in complete disagreement about, and we decided to try to agree on it during the kickoff.

The method as such appears quite simple, but with powerful results: The group gathers in a room. Everybody takes turns speaking about what is important to him or her about the issue, under a time limit of sixty seconds. (It could be forty-five, it could be ninety, but should be thereabouts. Somebody is assigned to use a stopwatch to time the speaking slots.) Everybody can spend his or her sixty seconds however he or she likes: by speaking about the issue at hand, by sitting in silence, by singing an unrelated song, or by dropping to the floor doing push-ups. The idea is that everybody will be discussing the issue, but the point is that each person can spend his or her time slot as he or she likes, and may not be interrupted by anyone during that time slot. Again, empower people. But once the sixty seconds are up, it's the next person's turn, going in a circle around the room in one direction of the circle, starting over on coming full circle and giving everybody another time slot, until everybody is in agreement on the issue at hand.

Here's the important part: everybody has the power of veto over a final decision. One single "no" from any participant is a final "no" for the group as a whole. Therefore, *nobody will leave the room as a loser.* This creates two very powerful mechanisms: the first is that it forces everybody to find a solution that is acceptable to everybody, and the second is that it slowly releases all fears of leaving the room as a loser, creating a completely different mind-set from the one surfacing when fighting internally.

It is equally important that everybody respects this and doesn't use any kind of peer pressure whatsoever to make somebody not exercise his or her right of veto. Everybody in the room has the power to block the final decision, and it is everybody's responsibility to find a solution that isn't blocked by anyone. Any attempts to belittle somebody's right to block a decision must be immediately stopped, reinforcing the respect for everybody's power of veto and the equality in the room.

When we discussed the issue in question in this large group of twenty-five people in the Swedish Pirate Party, it took two full rounds of speaking to see a complete transformation in attitude.

Those who had come into the room prepared to stall, fight, and delay a decision out of fear of losing had lost all such sentiments, and displayed inclusion in the decision-making process. This, in turn, made the decision making take considerably *less* time than if we had used a traditional voting method, even when starting from ridiculously diverse viewpoints and giving everybody the power of veto.

Seeing this transformation of attitude happen in the room — going from a tense, jaw-biting fear of losing and infighting to one of inclusion and a constructive mind-set — was a complete epiphany for me. It was so powerful you could taste it in the air.

> "WOW, I NEVER THOUGHT THIS WAS POSSIBLE. I WAS CONVINCED WE WOULD BE TEARING EACH OTHER'S THROATS OUT."
>
> — *A PARTICIPANT IN THE EVENT*

There's one more important thing to the consensus circle method: a final decision must not be proposed until it appears absolutely certain that the group will accept it, that nobody will exercise his or her right to veto. If just one person blocks the final decision, the issue may not be discussed any more that day, and the group will not have reached a decision. This is important, as any deviation

166

from this rule would throw the group right back into a factionalizing trench-warfare mind-set.

Now, this method doesn't solve the problem of how to define the group in question where everybody gets the power of veto. That will be a problem that depends heavily on the very specific situation and context.

## ORGANIZATIONAL ASTRONAUTS

Let's jump to another issue. From the very first day of the swarm, you will have people who claim that the swarm would work much better if it were organized in their favorite manner. More often than not, these people will fall into one of two categories.

The first category is technical people, who see everything as technical building blocks. Everything is logical in their world and can be moved around to achieve different, predictable results. As we have discussed, this way of looking at activists collides completely with swarmthink: activists are first and foremost *people*, and won't lend themselves to being moved around in some kind of arbitrary logical structure. They make friends and change the world, and that's it. The swarm is there to support their making friends and changing the world, not to fit them into a flowchart. The technical people eager to put things into comprehensive boxes will not perceive the swarm as a valid organization at all, as there is a lack of understandable, logical rules, and will seek to *fix* it by constraining people to roles and duties.

---

 Activists make friends and change the world, and that's it, from their perspective.

---

(The lack of understandable, logical rules comes from the simple fact that people are neither understandable nor logical by nature. They are social and passionate.)

The second dangerous type of wannabe "fixers" is the MBA-type people, who can come from large corporations or other bureaucratic institutions (including NGOs with strict internal democracy rules), and who will insist that the swarm must reshape to fit their preconceptions of an organization. The actions of these people roughly fit the saying that "when all you have is a hammer, everything looks like a nail"; they have seen one way of building an organization that has become *the* way in their minds. Therefore, this group of people will also regard the swarm as a nonorganization, an invalid organization, something that needs to be *fixed*, again.

There will be no shortage of people who want to reorganize — or even *organize*, as they will call it. I call these people "organizational astronauts" derogatorily and intentionally, as they will have missed that any organization at its core is about *people*, and the more you can use the way people behave naturally to further the swarm's goals, the faster you move.

The swarm is a *disorganization* by design. Some would prefer to call it a self-organization. In either case, there's nobody assigning everybody to boxes, tasks, and activities. That's why the organization works so well. Organizing it in the manner of organizational astronauts kills the swarm's ability to function as a swarm.

You need to make absolutely clear to these people that the swarm works by its own consensus, that decisions are made organically by individual activists flowing to and from initiatives of their own accord, and that this swarm is *your* initiative; if the wannabe fixers and organizational astronauts don't want to play by the swarm's rules, they need to use the law of two feet themselves, and go somewhere else.

---

 Watch out for organizational astronauts that want to "fix" the organization.

---

The swarm's rules, by the way, are by and large that there are no rules. These people will seek to impose them.

## DIVIDING SCARCE RESOURCES

This brings us to the delicate question of scarce resources in the swarm. As it grows, people will start to donate resources to it — servers, money, equipment. If it is a successful swarm, it will have recurring donations and some sort of predictable income.

In accordance with the overall theme of this chapter, some people will insist on "democratic control" over these resources. But again, doing so will turn the swarm into something it is not — there are no formal mechanisms for collective decisions, and there should not be. There are senses of rough consensus created by activists moving between initiatives.

At the end of the day, we have a structure that can handle budgets and money, and that is the supporting scaffolding structure we discussed in chapter 3. It becomes the duty of the officers of the swarm to distribute resources in the most effective way to support the end goals through the initiatives of the activists.

In this particular aspect, the swarm will resemble a traditional top-down organization in terms of allocating its resources in a decentralized manner. You, in control of the swarm's formal name and resources, allocate budgets to officers, who subdivide their budget in turn.

With this said, once the swarm has any money to speak of, a sizeable chunk of it should be devoted to supporting individual activists' initiatives where they can reclaim expenses. The swarm lives and dies with the creativity and initiatives of its activists.

## REWARDING PEOPLE

The military hands out medals when somebody does something good. This works in an impersonal organization, but a swarm is built on social bonds. So screw medals. Screw shiny trinkets. We can use much more subtle, and effective, ways to reward people in the swarm.

The key thing to rewards from a leadership position is to understand that *attention is reward*. If you are yelling at somebody who did something bad, you are giving him or her attention, and he or she will adapt his or her behavior to get more attention of the yelling kind. If you are praising somebody who did something good, he or she will adapt his or her behavior to get more attention of the praising kind.

(Now, as we recall from previous chapters, we should not be yelling at people in the first place in a swarm. If we do, people will copy our behavior, and disrespect for others will become an organizational value. A yelling match may be a fun game in the sauna between drunk college students, but it is not a very effective way of running an organization with tens of thousands of volunteers. Rather, I mention it here just to illustrate the point.)

It follows that we reward exemplary activist behavior with our attention, and completely ignore things that we want to see less of. Anything that we focus on in the swarm, for whatever reason, will grow in the swarm. Therefore, if there are behaviors we don't want to see growing, we should ideally pretend they aren't even there — block them out from our conscious radar, and spend time rewarding other kinds of behavior.

---

 Everything that we focus on, no matter how or why, will grow in the swarm.

---

So what behavior do we want to see growing?

Initiatives. Even initiatives that fail.

Supporting others. Actually, this one is quite important. I frequently emphasize that helping others excel is just as valuable as excelling on your own.

Creativity and sharing ideas.

Helping people get along.

While these are just examples, the criteria for rewards tend to converge on three key factors — helping the energy, the focus, and the passion of the swarm.

## TAMPERING WITH THE GOAL OF THE SWARM

At some point, you may want to adjust the goals of the swarm. For a political party, this is almost inevitable. For a single-issue swarm, it is more avoidable. Nevertheless, it creates very difficult problems in the face of the swarm's disorganization.

In a traditional corporation, this would have happened by executive decree. In a traditional NGO or government, it would have happened by majority vote. How does it happen in a swarm?

Let's go back to where we discussed motivations of fear. People who invest their time and identity in the swarm do so because they agree with the swarm on a fundamental social level. If the swarm reidentifies itself, that will create a discomfort. Even the aired idea of doing so will create severe discomfort among activists and cause a standstill and a halt to recruiting.

Say, for instance, that you have a swarm focused on going to Mars, and all of a sudden, you air the idea of repurposing the organization to selling mayonnaise instead, and skipping that Mars thing. Arguably, this is a ridiculous example to make a point, but the social and emotional effects will be very similar for the more credible repurposings — even those you think would make perfect sense.

After all, people have joined you in the swarm to accomplish something specific. If the reason they joined no longer exists, what are they doing in the swarm? What are they going to do with all the friendships they have built? What about all the energy and identity vested in the swarm? This creates a fundamental energy crisis with the swarm and an identity crisis with activists who have joined the swarm.

For this reason, if you should ever need to repurpose or regoal the swarm, you need to get a very high level of buy-in for this. You need to be aware that there will be a high degree of pushback, as your new goal or method isn't why people have joined. The costs will be high, but sometimes, it will also be the only way through, if the swarm has learned that the initially pictured goals or methods for attaining them weren't possible.

In such a scenario, voting may be the only way through. In doing so, you *will* create losers, many of whom will leave the swarm permanently with a bitter aftertaste. But if the alternative is to accept the failure of the swarm as a whole, it is still the preferable option.

## MEETINGS REVISITED

So at some extreme scenarios, you may still have to use voting. This, I really want to emphasize, should be a last resort through a conscious choice of options that best care for the energy, focus, and inclusiveness of the swarm, given a difficult circumstance, rather than just the default lazy option which is used "just because." In almost all cases, other mechanisms of conflict resolution are superior, far superior.

This brings up a number of problems. How do you determine who has the right to vote in a loose network? Everybody who wants to? Everybody who has left his or her contact details as an activist? Anybody who is a paid-up member of something? The last option will certainly be perceived as offensive to a lot of activists, for example — that influence can and must be *bought and paid for,* rather than deserved through effort and ideas, which is the swarm way.

In such a process, it is absolutely imperative that everybody is feeling included. This sounds easier than it is.

There are many ways to exclude people in practice from influencing the final outcome. If you call a physical meeting in a specific location, you exclude the people who are unable to get to that location on that time, for whatever reason. If you choose to discuss and vote during several hours on a Saturday, you are excluding parents who prefer to spend time with their kids. If you instead pick evening hours on weekdays, you will exclude people who work late. If the issue to vote on is reasonably complex, you are excluding people who can't take themselves the time to absorb the details of it.

It's easy to inadvertently exclude people from participation. Work to include.

Every exclusion is a failure. Just because you don't *see* any people being formally excluded, that doesn't mean people don't *feel* excluded. Every exclusion is a failure.

One way of getting around this, which the German Pirate Party has used very successfully, is to allow everybody with formal voting rights to select somebody to vote in his or her place. This voting right can be assigned differently for different issues, and also be assigned in turn, creating a chain of trust to make an informed vote. This taps into the heart of the swarm's social mechanisms of trusting people and friends, rather than fearing to lose. "Trust over fear." We like that. That's swarmthink. The German Pirate Party calls this *liquid democracy*.

Under this system, somebody could be voting for 1,337 people — herself and 1,336 other people who all have delegated their vote to that person, possibly in several steps. This makes the other 1,336 feel a level of inclusion and influence, even if they can't attend the discussion or vote — or, frankly, if they would rather be doing activism than administration.

However, the concept of liquid democracy doesn't solve the problem of determining who should have voting rights in the first place.

## DEALING WITH MAVERICKS

In the process of running the organization, you will occasionally discover people who don't feel they get enough attention from you personally for their ideas on how to run the swarm. (Attention is reward. They feel they're not rewarded enough.) This is quite likely due to you simply disagreeing with their ideas and not wanting to nurture them.

A particular kind of attention-craving maverick will create a group of followers determined to wreak havoc until they get their way. This can be very disruptive and goes counter to swarmthink, where the best ideas and the best arguments win, rather than the loudest mouths. Still, it is a significant disturbance.

The way to deal with this is not to agree to demands — if you do cave in to get rid of the disturbance, you will teach the entire organization that creating loud disturbances is a very effective way of getting influence in the swarm, and you will start going down a very bumpy road as other people start imitating that behavior. You will never be able to convince the maverick that he or she has bad ideas (and especially so if all he or she wants in the first place is attention for his or her person, rather than recognition for ideas). You will never be able to win that person.

An organization is people, and attention is reward.

Rather, you need to identify the reward mechanisms within the subgroup that has formed around the maverick. Odds are that they're forming a group identity around not being recognized as individual activists. You can shatter this identity by recognizing good contributors in the group who are hang-arounds of the maverick; odds are that there are several good contributors in that group who are just temporarily wooed by the maverick's charisma. If you pick away a couple of key people in this group and recognize them for good earlier work — unrelated to the maverick's yells — you will isolate the maverick, and the disturbance will lose critical mass.

Always remember that an organization is people, and that attention is reward.

*April 17, 2009, at 11 a.m.*

*We are gathered on the premises of the Stockholm District Court. The verdict against the two operators of the Pirate Bay, plus its media spokesperson and a fourth unrelated person, will be announced today at 11. It's been a race the entire week — this is the news everybody wants to communicate to their own audience first. Several tech magazines have created services that will send you a phone text as soon as the verdict has been announced. We will do that for our members, too. This is a matter of being fastest to report.*

*The lobby of the District Court is filled to capacity with reporters and pirates. Mostly reporters. Strangely, there is nobody from our adversaries — the copyright industry's lobby — present.*

*At 11 a.m. sharp, piles of prints of the verdict roll out into the lobby on trolleys. One of our activists, Jonathan, snags a copy immediately and rushes it to the table where the rest of us are gathered.*

*…One year in prison and thirty-five million SEK (about four million euros) in damages? Are they insane?*

*First things first. Press release and texts to our own. First, the press release. We load up the prepared "guilty" version of our press release, fill in the blanks...one year in prison...35 million...a few seconds of quick eyes for consistency...go. Send! OK, the press release is out. Next, phone texts. I quickly type a summary that fits in 140 characters and hit "Send," then turn around to face the press.*

*We are furious.*

*For the full next thirty minutes, the present senior people from the Pirate Party are giving back-to-back interviews to Swedish and international TV crews. All five of us, each before cameras in sequence. The press crews are lining up to get comments from us. The copyright industry lobby is nowhere to be found.*

*The media pressure is intense. As the ad-hoc interviews wrap up, and the TV crews leave to cut their footage for broadcast, the calls and pre-agreed slots for comments for interviews start at 12. To illustrate the pressure, I get a call from the BBC and have to tell them that I only have two minutes to give comments, as I have promised CNN a ten-minute slot in two minutes. They're grateful for the two minutes of comments and take the opportunity.*

*We are smart to have planned ahead and have already arranged for a rally permit tomorrow, "just in case," in one of Stockholm's largest squares. As the news spreads, people are absolutely furious over the injustice committed by the District Court. That rally permit will most definitely be needed — you won't be able to keep people off the streets. Our member count is spiking — it will triple over the next week, from 14,400 to 42,000. We're getting over 1,000 new members to the Pirate Party per hour.*

*As the immediate media pressure subsides, the people from the Pirate Party at the District Court are all in agreement, seeing the public opinion go stratospheric and beyond with rage: this egregious injustice was the Pirate Party's ticket to the European Parliament. We have said for three and a half years that things are this bad, we have told people this message everywhere we've had a voice, but almost nobody believed us. Now, they see for themselves that we were right all along, and they are furious about it. The European elections are just six weeks out. Voter memory may be said to be short, but it is certainly not that short.*

*We press ahead with our contingency plans and announce the protest rally tomorrow. News of our planned protest spreads quickly. It gathers people of all political colors.*

*As the next day breaks, and I take the stage on a large square filled to the brim with angry people, I open my speech: "The establishment has just declared war on an entire generation."*

# CHAPTER SEVEN

# Surviving Growth Unlike Anything the MBAs Have Seen

Following a high-profile event, your swarm just tripled in size in a week. You have twenty thousand new activists — new colleagues — that are all waiting for instructions from you, personally. They're waiting for instructions from you because your name is the only one they know of. There are no MBA classes on how to handle this situation: those people talk about the challenges you encounter when growing by more than 10 percent a year. This is how you handle 200 percent growth in a week.

On May 31, 2006, the Swedish police conducted a vastly overforceful raid against the Pirate Bay, creating tons of collateral damage and constitutional violations. Amid the protests, the Pirate Party tripled in member size, from the nascent 2,200 to the less-nascent 6,600 in a week. If you were looking at the member count graphs, it was as if the pilot of the graph pen had just pulled the stick backward and gone vertical. We called this a *verticality* and imagined it typically only happens once — a miracle-type event.

(We would have more than tripled if our servers had been able to handle the influx of new members. They had never been tested for this kind of load.)

On April 17, 2009, the verdict against the two operators of the Pirate Bay, its media spokesperson, and a fourth unrelated person was issued. It was seen as a gross miscarriage of justice. Amid the protests, the Pirate Party tripled in member count again, from 14,400 to becoming the third-largest Swedish party with 42,000 members in a week. The party had just had its second verticality.

Getting 20,000 new colleagues and activists in a week isn't a pipe dream. It happens. Quite rarely, but it does happen. You need to be prepared for it.

## BROADCASTING AND MAINTAINING VALUES

Common organizational practice holds that you should write down your organization's values. This is not enough in a fast-growing swarm; you need to do three more things.

A values document is usually part of or joined with a corporate mission statement, and is one of many write-only documents (meaning that they are never actually *read* by anyone) in a typical organization, along with environmental policy, diversity policy, and laundry schedule. (To be honest, the laundry schedule may not belong on the list, as it is typically read once in a while.) However, in a swarm organization, the organizational culture cannot be communicated from person to person as the organization grows — it must be actively communicated centrally, and *repeatedly* communicated as new people keep joining.

Let's take a look at a sample values document — this one is, again, from the Pirate Party, so you will note that there is mention of a General Assembly, which probably won't be present in a nonpolitical swarm:

# A SAMPLE VALUES DOCUMENT

Our organization is built on three different pillars: swarm work, traditional NGO structures, and a hierarchical top-down structure that distributes resources to support the swarm. These are roughly equally important, but fill completely different needs: the traditional NGO structure only resides at the General Assembly and the party board level, for the party's legal foundation as an nonprofit organization; the hierarchic work distribute resources and associated mandates from the board into the organization, making decisions for effective opinion building and other operative work; and the spontaneous swarm work is the backbone of our activism.

We work under the following principles:

**We make decisions.** We aren't afraid to try out new things, new ways to shape opinion and drive the public debate. We make decisions without asking anybody's permission, and we stand for them. Sometimes, things go wrong. It's always okay to make a mistake in the Pirate Party, as long as one is capable of learning from that mistake. Here's where the famous "three-pirate rule" comes into play: if three self-identified pirates are in agreement that some kind of activism is beneficial to the party, they have authority to act in the party's name. They can even be reimbursed for expenses related to such activism, as long as it is reasonable (wood sticks, glue, and paint are reasonable; computer equipment and jumbotrons are not).

**We are courageous.** If something goes horribly wrong, we deal with it then, and only then. We are never nervous in advance. Everything can go wrong, and everything can go right. We are allowed to do the wrong thing, because otherwise, we can never do the right thing either.

**We advance one another.** We depend on our cohesion. It is just as much an achievement to show solitary brilliance in results as it is to advance other activists or officers.

**We trust one another.** We know that each and every one of us wants the best for the Pirate Party.

**We take initiatives and respect those of others.** The person who takes an initiative gets it most of the time. We avoid criticizing the initiatives of others, for they who take initiatives do something for the party. If we think the initiative is pulling the party in the wrong direction, we compensate by taking an initiative of our own more in line with our own ideals. If we see something we dislike, we respond by making and spreading something we like, instead of pointing out what we dislike. We need diversity in our activism and strive for it.

**We respect knowledge.** In discussing a subject, any subject, hard measured data is preferable. Second preference goes to a person with experience in the subject. Knowing and having experience take precedence before thinking and feeling, and hard data takes precedence before knowing.

**We respect the time of others and the focus of the organization.** If we dislike some activity or some decision, we discuss, we argue, we disagree, and/or we start an initiative of our own that we prefer. On the other hand, starting or supporting an emotional conflict with a negative focus, and seeking quantity for such a line of conflict, harms the organization as a whole and drains focus, energy, and enthusiasm from the external, opinion-shaping activities. Instead, we respect the time and focus of our co-activists, and the focus of the organization. When we see the embryo of an internal conflict, we dampen it by encouraging positive communication. When we see something we dislike, we produce and distribute something we like. We work actively to spread love and respect, and to dampen aggression and distrust. We communicate positively. If we see a decision we dislike, we make our point about why we dislike it without provoking feelings, or, better yet, we explain why an alternative would be better. We campaign outward and cohesively, not inward and divisively. Again, we communicate positively.

**We act with dignity.** We're always showing respect in our shaping of public opinion: respect toward each other, toward newcomers, and toward our adversaries. We act with courtesy, calm, and factuality, both on and off the record. In particular, we're never disrespectful against our co-activists (one of the few things that officers in the Pirate Party will have zero tolerance with).

**We're in parliament.** We behave like the parliamentary party that we are. Related to the point above.

**We are long term.** We depend on making the 2010 and 2014 elections, so our work is long term. As in "on a time span of several years." The time span between elections, four years, is practically a geological era for many of us net activists.

**We represent ourselves.** The Pirate Party depends on a diversity of voices. None of us represents the Pirate Party on blogs and similar: we're a multitude of individuals that are self-identified pirates. The diversity gives us our base for activism, and multiple role models build a broader recruitment and inspiration base for activism. Internally, we're also just ourselves, and never claim to speak for a larger group: if our ideas get traction, that's enough; if they don't get traction, the number of people agreeing with those ideas is irrelevant.

You should keep reminding the entire swarm about the organization values regularly, as part of your heartbeat messages, which we'll be discussing in the next chapter — both to reinforce the values to old activists and to introduce them to new activists. Describe one value in every or every other heartbeat message. Needless to say, you also need to practice what you preach.

However, having this document and continuously reminding people that it exists, in words and in action, is not enough. You also need *leadership guidance* and tons of *empty positions* in the organization that new activists can fill, as we discussed in chapter 3. As part of a surge like the ones described, you may discover that your organization has recruited an assistant local media manager in Buckabeyond, Backwater, Ohio. If you don't have an empty box for that position in advance, it can't be filled. If the officers of the swarm's scaffolding don't know how to uphold and communicate the swarm values, it won't happen.

So in addition to the values that go for the organization as a whole, you also need to communicate values for the leaders that take on formal responsibility in the scaffolding. Just like the overall values that apply to all activists, these need to be communicated over and over, and, of course, reinforced through action.

Here's a sample set of leadership values for a working swarm.

## A SAMPLE LEADERSHIP DOCUMENT

Leading in the Pirate Party is a hard but rewarding challenge. It's considerably harder than being a middle manager in a random corporation. On the other hand, it's somewhat easier than sending letters by carrier mackerel across the Sahara. Above all, it is stimulating, exciting, and simply quite fun.

The challenges lie in the constant demands for transparency and influence from your area of responsibility, combined with the demands for results and accountability from those you report to. Basically, this means that leadership in the Pirate Party is a social skill, rather than a management or technical skill. It is about making people feel secure in their roles.

Above all, we need to defend two things in all our actions:

— The organization's *focus*. We're going to make the parliamentary threshold. Everything we do must be aimed at that.

— The organization's *energy*. It is incredibly easy to get drained of energy if you start feeling negative vibes. There is a need for a constantly reinforced we-can-do-this sentiment.

In order to sustain these two values, we who have taken on officers' and leaders' responsibility use the following means:

**Monkey see, monkey do.** We are role models. We act just the way we want other people in the organization to act. One part of this is to always try to be positive. In all organizations, the organization as a whole will copy its officers and leaders. When we yell at somebody, we spread the culture of yelling at one another. When we advance and praise people for what they do, we spread the culture that people should advance and praise one another. Therefore, we do the latter.

This can be hard. An example is in forums where we find ourselves in a discussion with somebody who seems to be wrong. It's easy to take on an irritated tone of voice and use condescending language (for a funny illustration of this phenomenon, look up the URL *http://xkcd.com/386/*). We must avoid this by being aware of the risk and counteracting it. This goes especially for net-only communication, where important parts of communication such as body language, emphasis, and tone of voice just disappear, parts that would otherwise have reduced the experienced aggression in many comment fields. Attitudes are highly contagious, so, therefore, we make sure to have a positive and understanding attitude. We spread love, trust, energy, and enthusiasm.

**We make decisions.** We have had decision-making authority delegated to us in some area of the organization, and we use it. We are not afraid of saying, "I make this decision," because it is our express and explicit task to make decisions independently and then stand for them. The opposite would be if we let everybody have a say in everything. We don't operate like that. We make decisions by ourselves; we have standalone decision makers. You are one of them. Also, we avoid voting to the extreme and only use it as a very last resort: voting creates losers.

However, our being decision makers is no excuse for treating the mandate with disrespect. We treat everybody affected by our decisions with just as much respect as we need ourselves to keep enjoying respect as leaders and decision makers. Decisions shall be used to strengthen the organization's energy and focus, and a decision that makes harmfully large portions of the organization upset about the decision in itself should be rescinded. This calls for an independent striking of a balance between making independent decisions and our dependence on the trust of the affected to keep making decisions, and the grayscale is quite large.

**We lead by inspiring and suggesting, never by commanding.** In a swarm, nobody can or should be told what to do. We do not have any kind of mandate to point at people and tell them to do things. Rather, we must inspire them to greatness. We cause things to happen by saying aloud that "I'm going to do X, because I think it will accomplish Y. If enough of us do this, we could probably cause Z to happen. Therefore, it would be nice to have some company when I do X," or something along those lines in our own words.

**We advance role models.** We reward our colleagues as often as we can, both in public and private, when they display a behavior we want to reinforce. In particular, this goes for activists who advance their colleagues. We praise and reward individual brilliance as much as helping others to shine. This is important.

**We reward with attention.** Every behavior that gets attention in an organization is reinforced. Therefore, we focus and give attention to good behavior, and, as far as possible, we completely ignore bad behavior. We praise the good and ignore the bad (with one exception below).

**We assume good faith.** We assume that everybody wants the organization to succeed, even when they do things we don't understand. We assume they act out of a desire to help the Pirate Party, even if we perceive the result as directly opposite. In such situations, we show patience and encourage activism while helping newcomers make themselves comfortable in our organizational culture. In such a manner, we also display good faith ourselves as leaders and act as role models.

**We react immediately against disrespect.** Even if we have great tolerance for mistakes and bad judgment, we do not show tolerance when somebody shows disrespect toward his or her colleagues, toward other activists. Condescending argumentation or other forms of behavior used to suppress a co-activist is never accepted. When we see such behavior, we jump on it and mark it as unacceptable. In our leadership roles, we have an important role in making sure that people feel secure in their roles, with no bullying accepted. If the bully continues despite having the behavior pointed out, he or she will be shut out from the area where he or she disrespects his or her peers, and if some friend reinvites him or her back just for spite, we will probably shut off the friend, too. We have absolute-zero tolerance for disrespect or intentionally bad behavior against co-activists.

**We speak from our own position.** When we perceive somebody as being in the wrong, we never say "you're stupid" or similar, but start from our own thoughts, feelings, and reactions. We communicate using the model "When you perform action X, I feel Y, since I perceive you think Z," possibly with the addition "I had expected A or B." An example: "When you give the entire budget to activism, I feel frustrated, as I feel you ignore our needs for IT operations. I had expected you to ask how much it costs to run our servers." This creates a constructive dialogue instead of a confrontational one.

**We stand for our opinions.** We never say "Many people feel…" or try to hide behind some kind of quantity of people. Our opinions are always and only our own, and we stand for them. The one exception is when we represent an organization in a protocolled decision.

**Administration is a support and never a purpose.** We try to keep administrative weight and actions to a minimum, and instead prioritize activism. It is incredibly easy to get stuck in a continuously self-reinforcing bureaucratic structure, and every formal action or process needs to be regularly questioned to evaluate how it helps activism and shaping the public opinion.

**We build social connections.** We meet, and we make others meet. Social connections — that people meet, eat, and have beer or coffee with each other — are what make the Pirate Party into an organization.

**We develop our colleagues.** We help everybody develop and improve, both as activists and leaders. Nobody is born with leadership; it is an acquired skill. We help each other develop our skills, even in our roles as officers and leaders.

Finally, all leaders and decision makers in the Pirate Party should see the fifty-five-minute video "How to protect your open source project from poisonous people." On the surface, it is about a technical project, but the focus is on courses of action when events pop up that disturb the focus or energy in a volunteer community. It is very applicable to our organization, too.

This is a document that is being updated as we go. It cannot be used to beat somebody over the head because a certain part can be read a certain way: the important thing is the spirit and not the letter.

These two sample documents, taken together, sum up a lot of this book.

## DECENTRALIZED LEADERSHIP, EMPTY BOXES

This leads us to what happens when you do get a *verticality* with a sudden tripling of the activist base. On average, every officer in the swarm's scaffolding will need to appoint two more officers. This requires two things:

First, it requires officers and leaders who are comfortable with appointing other officers and delegating authority over resources and responsibilities, or even taking on deputies or assistants. They need to have the authority to do this independently, and they have to *know* that they have this authority and are *expected* to use it. There is no way that you or anyone else will be able to take a bottleneck position and still seize this moment. (You shouldn't have a bottleneck position in the first place, so that particular problem should not materialize.)

Second, it requires empty boxes in the organizational chart of the scaffolding. Tons and tons of empty boxes everywhere. So don't be afraid of populating the entire set of empty boxes at the organization's genesis moment, even if just a few at the top (or center, depending on your point of view) will have names in them at the start, as we discussed in chapter 3.

## GROW WITH HAVING FUN

In the context of growing, having fun in the organization is more important than just having fun at work. It is crucial to growing the activist base.

The reason is simple: people gravitate to other people who seem to be enjoying themselves. If you are having fun, more people will want to join you. If you are bickering and infighting, people who would otherwise be potential activist recruits will instead walk an extra mile around you to avoid being drawn in.

 Having fun in the swarm is crucial to growing the activist base.

Having fun in the organization is crucial to success. You need to make sure that you and your colleagues, all several thousand of them, have fun.

## GRINDING, GRINDING, GRINDING

Success in a swarm doesn't happen smoothly and fluidly. It happens in hard-to-predict enormous bursts.

You may have spoken about a subject for a good year or two, seeing no return on your efforts at all. Then, something happens, and more or less overnight, tens of thousands of people realize you have been right all along and join your swarm for the fight.

While grinding along without seeing any returns can feel disheartening at times, it's important to understand that people are listening and do take notice to what you're saying. They're just choosing to not act on it at the time being — maybe because it's not important to them, maybe because they plainly don't believe a word you say.

Then, all of a sudden, the government announces new horrible legislation that confirms everything you've been saying for the past two years, and you find yourself with twenty thousand new followers and five thousand new activists overnight, as you've gone from a doomsday prophet to being a rallying point for well-needed change. That's the way it works.

The first part of the challenge is to drum up your own motivation to keep grinding, grinding, grinding, even when seeing little to no visible return. Write those articles and op-eds, stage those events, keep handing out those flyers, even in an emotional wintertime. People *are* taking notice.

The second part of the challenge is to immediately get out of grinding mode when this catalyzing event happens, and go into an intense recruitment mode to take care of all the new activists, as described in this chapter. Then, as the recruitment burst fades, you teach all the new activists to grind public opinion in the same way as you had been doing, the swarm now having a much larger surface area than before the growth burst.

However, we should not confuse persistent day-to-day grinding with a refusal to see roadblocks for the uptake of the swarm's ideas. If people tell you that your website is confusing, that the officers of the swarm are inaccessible, or that new people who come to gatherings aren't feeling welcome, those are real issues and should absolutely not be taken as a sign to just keep doing what you're already doing. Everybody needs to listen for real blocks to adoption of the swarm's ideas, all the time — but it's when there are no such blocks coming, and there's still no momentum, that everyday motivation can be hard to muster up. It is precisely at this point that one must keep grinding.

## MAINTAIN ONE VALUE SET, ONE VALUE BASE

So far, this book has focused a lot on success recipes, but it can be equally instructing to learn from failures. My greatest strategic mistake ever was one of greed, as is often the case. It involves the founding of the youth wing of the Pirate Party — the *Ung Pirat* ("Young Pirate").

(In Europe, political parties almost always have youth wings, where teenagers learn about policies and values of the party from their similarly aged peers. While this would seem odd in many parts of the world, it is perfectly normal in Europe and Sweden.)

I was informed that the party and movement could collect hundreds of thousands of euros a year in governmental grants by founding a youth wing: the government awards yearly grants for youth activity that gives young people a meaningful pastime, and political activity falls well within that scope. Knowing how cash strapped the party was, my first mistake in this sequence was getting blinded by the prospect of money, and not learning enough about the subject.

The people who volunteered to bootstrap the youth wing were very good at what they did, as is typical for a swarm, and had considerable experience with the subject. They knew exactly what red tape to avoid and how to optimize the youth wing's structure in advance to pass through all the hoops and jump over all the pits to get on the fast track for youth activity grants.

Here's the second problem, which is one I wasn't aware of at the time, but which was my second grave mistake. The government places rigorous demands on the organizational structure of a youth organization to be eligible for grants — among other things, it must be strictly democratic with tons of red tape and voting, which goes completely counter to what we learned about swarmwise conflict resolution methods in chapter 6. In general, you could say that it must fit the 1960s model of a nonprofit organization to be eligible for grants.

Now, as we recall, if you have that kind of structure, you suppress the diversity which is required for a swarm to succeed. Furthermore, it encourages internal conflict, as that is how decisions are made when everything goes to a vote — and, by extension, it builds skills in such internal conflict, rather than skills in working swarmwisely.

At this point, still unaware of the problems ahead, I made my third and crucial mistake and connected the recruitment function of the Pirate Party with that of its youth wing. Youth grants are measured on the number of members below twenty-six years of age plus the number of local chapters, and the youth wing was optimized to maximize these numbers. Therefore, the youth wing was bootstrapped with the existing young members of the party, and every new member to the party got the option to click "I'm under twenty-six and want to join the youth wing, too" on joining. I'd soon come to understand what a mistake this had been — yes, it brought money to the movement, but the strategic damage was far worse.

The youth wing became eligible for governmental grants on January 16, 2009, which was a record time from its founding in December 2006 to its eligibility for youth activity grants. The people setting it up exactly as I had asked had performed in record time for Sweden's grant bureaucracy, which — again — is typical for a swarm (although a fair amount of credit must be attributed to the individual skill sets, too).

However, as we learned in chapter 5, people will self-organize to improve anything you measure in public. The youth wing was built to optimize its grant eligibility, and kept measuring those parameters in public. As a result, people kept building the youth wing in a way that was completely different from the party itself — and worse, in a way that was destructive to the party, should that kind of organizational thinking come to seep into it. And of course it did. The youth wing, after all, was supposed to be the primary activist base and recruitment grounds for the next generation of activists.

In this way, the bureaucratic rules for governmental youth activity grants in Sweden slowly came to poison the cooperative, diverse swarm mentality of the Pirate Party by means of controlling the structure of its youth wing.

Now, you could argue that the structure wasn't really *controlled* as such by the grant rules — but the point of founding the youth wing had been to comply with them to bring money to the movement, in a blind greed that caused heavy strategic damage.

Predictably, as we learned from chapter 5, the youth wing became increasingly focused on optimizing itself for the grants that fueled it. Moreover, using its superior resources, it was able to siphon new activists off into shapers of compliance with grant rules before the main party was able to train them into effective shapers of public opinion.

To make the problem far worse, a culture emerged — or was perhaps cultivated — in the youth wing where it considered its own organizational culture of internal conflict to be *far superior* to the swarmwise way of assisting each other in a culture of diversity, and actively tried to bring a culture of internal conflicts into the swarm organization of the party — blissfully unaware and ignorant that all its recruitment, and therefore resources, depended on the very swarm methodologies it disdained.

So the disaster here was threefold:

**One** — The youth wing had many times the resources of the party, and used them to train new activists in values of democratic infighting that were completely foreign to swarm activism, and to promote administration over activism, before the party could teach the new activists how swarm organizations work.

**Two** — Since the youth wing members were also members of the party, it was impossible to shut down the rerouting of members from the party to the youth wing. The executive part of the party organization ultimately got its mandate through the General Assembly, after all, where these people watched out for their interests of getting more money and resources.

**Three** — The youth wing would otherwise have been a natural activist training ground for the party; now, it had become a training ground for activists that would kill the values that had made the party successful. There was no discernible "outside" where you could recruit new activists that hadn't been already trained in swarm-killing methods and values.

So the youth wing was conflict driven, rather than consensus and activism driven. It was built on principles of infighting peacefully ("learning democratic principles") rather than principles of changing the world. It was built on promoting and rewarding administration over activism. It had taken a beachhead in the party's General Assembly that was impossible to undo and had control over the activist recruitment inflows, and the damage to the organization values was becoming greater by the day.

In order to illustrate in objective facts just how introvertedly the youth wing had been built, we can observe that in an election year (2010), the election in question was not mentioned in the activity plan for the year. Yes, you read that right: the organization supposed to be a primary activist base for a political party didn't care about an upcoming important election. It was a complete disaster, and it kept defending itself against being shut off from the recruitment flow of new activists which came from the mother party.

The people who had set up the youth wing exactly as I had asked had outperformed themselves and set up the best possible organization to match the specs and beyond, beating Swedish records in the process and indeed getting those hundreds of thousands of euros per year — but the strategic damage to the underlying values far outweighed the monetary gains.

As a final blow, the money wasn't allowed to go to the party at all, but had to stay in the youth wing.

The lesson here is that no millions of cash in the world — even if you do get them — can repair the damage to your organization if you lose your value base. This was my biggest strategic mistake ever. You must maintain *one*, and *only one*, value base.

 Don't ever risk trading your swarm culture for temporary cash. Keep one value base.

As of this writing, the recently elected head of the described youth wing is one of the strongest swarmthink activist spirits in the movement. It remains to be seen if the damage to the cooperative, diverse values can be undone for this particular swarm.

## SERIOUSLY, ONE POWER BASE

When I spoke to previous challenger parties across Sweden, they all bemoaned one specific organizational detail that had ultimately become their downfall: multiple power bases.

They had organized into several separate formal organizations, each with its own legal identity, each with responsibility for a particular geography or subgeography. This had several disastrous effects.

First, it vested activists in their local organization's interests, rather than in the swarm as a whole. Tons of energy was diverted from activism into internal power struggles between intentionally created factions. You want every activist to be part of the one swarm, rather than part of "the subswarm of Fort Duckburg fighting for its own interests against the subswarm of neighboring West Gotham." You don't want to intentionally create factions for infighting.

Second, it creates metric tons of administrative redundancy. You want as few people as possible doing administrative work, and as many as possible doing activism. Therefore, you want to centralize the administrative workload to one or a very few people, and reduce the workload of everybody else to be on the level of clicking on "give me a cash advance for this great event we're having." Having to deal with many legal identities means that each legal-identity organization must do its own bookkeeping, tax forms, recordkeeping, and so on, wasting many activist hours that would otherwise have gone toward activism.

Third, you want to keep the number of people who enjoy administration to a minimum, too. People who enjoy activism attract other people who also enjoy extroverted activism to the swarm. In contrast, if you let the number of administrators start to grow, they will attract more and more administrative bureaucrats, and worse, start repelling activism-minded people.

> THE MAN WHOSE LIFE IS DEVOTED TO PAPERWORK HAS LOST THE INITIATIVE. HE IS DEALING WITH THINGS THAT ARE BROUGHT TO HIS NOTICE, HAVING CEASED TO NOTICE ANYTHING FOR HIMSELF.
> — C NORTHCOTE PARKINSON

Fourth, and less important, it also creates a lot of unnecessary cost in redundancy — and that's for an already cash-strapped organization, as swarms tend to be. A bank account may cost fifty euros a year. For one organization, that's a digestible cost. For fifty legal identities, that's suddenly €2,500. Repeat for all other costs associated with being a standalone legal entity and multiply as needed.

As party leader of a challenger party, I spoke to people from previous challenger parties that had failed to understand where they went wrong. Every single challenger party I spoke to that had failed pointed out the creation of several parallel organizations with their own legal identity as the one reason, or one of the primary reasons, that the party had failed. There's an important lesson to learn from that.

So keep your swarm to being *one* legal entity (if you bother to make it a formal legal entity at all). Many brave attempts at changing the world have fallen on the intentional creating of internal factions, with results as predictable as the sun setting.

*April 29, 2009, in the early evening.*

*There are some phone calls you never forget. You can recall the smell, the ambient sounds, your exact position, your mood, everything about the situation as you are told some things. This is one such call.*

*As I am relaxing with my girlfriend with a glass of wine in the early evening, Christian Engström's name and face flash on the phone to the catchy election tune of "The pirates are sailing, with Brussels in sight." As I hit the green "take call" button, I casually answer "Yep?" Christian and I speak often. His voice comes on.*

*"This must absolutely not leak, but we're getting 5.1 percent in a poll that will be published tomorrow." Being the list topper for the European elections, he has been asked for a comment for tomorrow's news.*

*The world just stops. This is the piece of news I have been wanting to hear since January 1, 2006. This is the first time ever that we are on our own bar, polling at levels that would give us parliamentary seats. Polling above that parliamentary threshold for entry — 4 percent in Sweden — means that you can no longer be dismissed by antagonists as a joke party and a wasted vote: you are a serious contender, and you are expected to get elected.*

*We've been fighting for that exact recognition for three and a half years. The events of the past month were the catalyst we needed, with the despicable travesty of justice that was the trial against the Pirate Bay operators, its media spokesperson, and a fourth unrelated person.*

*The European elections are just five weeks out, and we are getting scores that would put us in the European Parliament for the first time. This means that the media would be speaking about us between now and the elections, through the entire advance voting period. The timing could not possibly have been better. The road to Brussels lies open.*

*It takes but an hour more before rumors start buzzing around the net of the Pirate Party getting 5 percent in the most recent poll, long before the publication date has broken. Trying discreetly to find out if somebody in the party has leaked the news prematurely, I learn quickly that geeks who were typesetting, printing, and distributing tomorrow's paper have been all over the news as well — you just can't contain such a happy message once the newspaper goes to print in multiple locations around the country.*

*Closer still to the election, we would be reported as the country's third largest party in polls. While this doesn't count for much in a country with a two-party system, the situation is completely different in a country with proportional representation like Sweden and most of Europe. In such countries, there are five to ten parties in Parliament, and some unknown coming from nowhere to become the third largest in seemingly a month is a really big deal.*

*Actually, scratch that. It's a big deal even if you do it in three and a half years.*

# PART III

## DELIVERING WITH THE SWARM

# CHAPTER EIGHT

# Using Social Dynamics to Their Full Potential

The key to a successful swarm is to be better at under-standing and using massive-scale social dynamics than your competitors. We've looked at some of the specific techniques in chapters 4 and 6. This chapter will round off with the more advanced, yet most crucial techniques.

When you communicate the swarm's goals to tens of thousands of people or even to hundreds of thousands, it poses unique challenges, as they're all in different positions of understanding the swarm's goals and have different motivations for choosing to receive your communications. You need to be aware of all of these and cater to the well initiated as well as the just-recruited activists, all at the same time.

## SOCIAL LINKS

A lot of communities make the mistake of only using online connections. As we observed in chapter 4 when taking to the streets,
the real strength of an activist swarm lies in being able to cross-use
online and offline social friendships.

 The real strength of the swarm comes from
cross-using online and offline friendships.

Offline friendships are much, much stronger than online friendships
and connections. It is the offline discussions we want to cover the
swarm's topics; they are much stronger in terms of emotional
attachment and intensity between people. Thus, we need to use the
reach of online tools and communication to make people want to
talk about the swarm's goals in their respective offline environments, where the possibility of recruiting new activists is much,
much better than on a random web page.

Once we've established that we want to utilize the offline friendships that activists have with their friends to explain the swarm's
message to more people, we need to look at how our activists are in
different situations with different abilities to do that.

## GROWING ON THE EDGES

A swarm only grows on its fuzzy outer edge: at the swarm's center, where you are, everybody is already involved at the highest activity level. This leads to an important insight: the people who are most active can't recruit any new activists to the swarm themselves by talking to their friends.

The people leading a swarm must be acutely aware that they cannot directly influence a single individual directly to join the swarm. The swarm can only grow at its edges, where people who have joined the swarm know people who have not yet joined. There, and only there, are there social links that can be used to communicate the values, mission, and enthusiasm of the swarm to gain new recruits.

But it is still the responsibility of the most motivated people to grow the swarm, despite the fact that they can't do so personally. Rather, it is their responsibility to enable the people who can recruit new people to do so, despite the fact that the people in a leading position have no idea who these people actually *are*.

## HEARTBEAT MESSAGES

To enable such recruitment at the edge, a couple of key components must be communicated to the entire swarm at regular intervals in *heartbeat messages*. This must be done by the people with the most experience in talking about the swarm, typically once a week. The heartbeat messages should contain at least the following:

**Newsflow.** Let people know what's going on, both in the swarm and in the world as it relates to the swarm. Both are equally important. The most active will already know most of it, but your wording of it will help them, too. Overcommunicate the context of the news, the external news in particular — make sure even the newest activists understand why you chose to highlight the events that you pick in the newsflow. Don't assume everybody read your letter from last week, because the newest activists didn't.

 Send a weekly letter with newsflow, sample rhetoric, urgency, and confidence.

**Sample rhetoric.** The newly joined people, who know the most not-yet-joined people, are also the ones who are the most insecure in their rhetoric about why the swarm is important, fun, and skilled in its work for a better world. Their confidence can be increased in many ways — one of the most straightforward and successful is to supply direct quotes that can initiate a conversation, or sample responses to typical questions.

**Confidence.** This brings me to the next point — the people who are in a position to recruit must also be supplied with the confidence to do so. One of the easiest ways is to enable them to use stickers or pins with the swarm's symbols that in turn lead to conversations like above. If they're not confident enough to initiate conversations, just identifying with the swarm gets part of the way there.

**Sense of urgency.** When these people are in a rhetorical and confident position to recruit new people to the swarm, they also need to want to do so. Telling them in a mass mailing is obviously not enough: they must actively want to recruit themselves. If they believe in the swarm and its mission, part of that mission must be to grow the swarm itself and to understand how such growth contributes to the swarm's end success.

A swarm grows by people talking to one another, one conversation at a time. The Swedish Pirate Party grew to fifty thousand members just like that: one person at a time, one conversation at a time.

These conversations are the key to the long-term success of the swarm.

## UNDERSTANDING THE ACTIVATION LADDER

In any swarm, it is essential to know where the paths to individual success coincide with the success of the swarm's mission, and to bring new recruits into alignment with one of these paths as soon as possible.

When somebody joins a swarm with a particular mission, he or she obviously doesn't go immediately from first hearing of the swarm to being its leader. There are many, many steps in between: hearing of the swarm for the first time, hearing again of the swarm, looking it up on the web, seeing somebody in the streets, talking to him or her, etc. This is obvious when spelled out, but for being so obvious, surprisingly few organizations respond to it. We call this the *activation ladder,* and the swarm must understand each step on the ladder and make it as easy as possible for everybody to climb to the next step of activation.

In the previous section, we discussed how the swarm can grow only on its edges. The activation ladder is equally important to understanding recruitment: the edges of the swarm are not sharp, but quite fuzzy, and it's hard to define the moment when people decide to activate themselves in the swarm for the first time. Is it when they hear about the swarm? When they visit its web pages? When they first contact a human being in the swarm? I would argue that all three of these are different steps on the activation ladder.

The key insight here is that from the center, where the people leading the swarm are located, the swarm looks like a *flat mesa* (with just one steep step to climb), but from the outside, it looks like a *rounded hill* (with many small steps). This is key to making it easy for people to move to the highly active center of the swarm: as we want to activate people in the swarm, it's important to understand that activation is a *gradual* process with many steps on the activation ladder.

 Activation is a gradual process with many steps on the activation ladder.

The crucial action that is needed from the people leading the swarm is to identify as many steps as possible on the activation ladder, and make each of these steps as easy and accessible as possible. Again, it sounds obvious, but many organizations fail miserably at this. Some swarms or formal organizations make it easy to become a member but explain nothing about what they do, while others go out of their way to explain how important the members are but make it impossible to come in contact with an officer of the swarm.

The problem with these organizations is usually that they have chosen one key metric that measures their success, and so, the organization reshapes to focus on that metric alone rather than the full activation ladder. (We discussed metrics a bit in chapter 5, as you will recall.)

There are several key things that need to be done. Some of the least obvious are to always make sure that all people in the swarm can respond meaningfully to questions about the swarm's purpose from people who are just hearing about the swarm — normal social growth should never be underestimated — and that there are always plenty of empty boxes in the organizational chart for people who want to take formal and real responsibility for the swarm's daily operations. Yes, we keep coming back to this detail, because it is important.

Apart from this, asking a dozen activists to describe each step that led them to join and activate should be a good start to discover the activation ladder for a particular swarm.

## MOBILIZING ACTIVISTS

The key success factor for any swarm is its ability to mobilize activists; its ability to activate its followers. As we saw in chapter 5, metrics are tremendously important to follow and track, and can be used successfully as a motivator for internal competitions and trendspotting alike.

When push comes to shove, it's not the number of Twitter followers, Facebook fans, or newsletter subscribers that counts (even though these metrics are easily measured). *It's how many people you can activate.* This is a different number, one that isn't as easily seen, even though it has some form of correlation to the easily measured numbers: it can be assumed to rise and fall when the other numbers rise and fall, but over and above that, it's hard to predict.

 The metric that matters is how many people you can mobilize to take action.

Also, it depends a lot on your leadership. As we saw in chapter 5, direct leadership will have a tremendously better effect at activating people *en masse* than vague wishes when it comes to doing something very specific.

But there's more to it than that. Your leadership is not enough. You must also provide the means for your officers and local leaders to activate people on their own. You may want a flash mob to form outside a courtroom as a verdict is handed out, for example, when all the TV cameras are there. You have twenty-five minutes, and you're in a different city. What do you do?

The first thing to realize is that *you* shouldn't do anything except contact the local leaders of the swarm and ask them to make something happen. The next thing to realize is that these local leaders must have the tools to make that something happen.

The Swedish Pirate Party has tools to send a text message to all activists in a geographical area. (We don't track the activists' actual location — that would be bad and rude behavior. Instead, people can subscribe to messages related to certain areas where they typically move about.) The local leader would go into our swarm activation tools, choose an area to blanket with a phone message to our activists' phones, and send something like "Flash mob for the verdict today. Meet up outside the District Court on 123 Such Street at 12:30, 22 minutes from now. Get there if you can."

When such a message is sent to thousands of phones, hundreds of people show up. That is more than sufficient to look like a significant group of people, especially if you make sure that placards are available from a nearby stash so that the group looks like, well, *a group* — your group — rather than just a random assorted audience.

Remember, a swarm can't compete on resources — but it is absolutely unbeatable on speed, reaction time, and cost efficiency.

## CALLS TO ARMS: PERCEPTION IS REALITY

You can and should use mass text messaging over your favorite platform to mobilize the swarm not just to physical locations, but to any place where your issues are discussed. This particularly includes comment fields and discussion threads.

A lot of people in general want to be on the winning team in most contexts and will adapt their behavior to match it. Therefore, if you can make your swarm *look* like the winning team, regardless of your actual strength, 90 percent of your work is done. In marketing, this principle is based on the mantra that "perception is reality" — in other words, what's real is what we *perceive* to be real. But the mechanisms go beyond that idea; perception also *shapes* reality.

In order to make the most of this, you need some kind of alert mechanism within your swarm to call for activists' attention whenever a certain idea, perspective, or product — the one your swarm is focused on — needs to dominate a discussion, a comment field, a forum thread, etc. The addition of a mere twenty-five people to the discussion who all are pulling in one specific direction can often make it look like public opinion is overwhelmingly in favor of your swarm's goals for somebody casually visiting the discussion — and for everybody writing in a particular thread, there are ninety-nine people just reading.

In the beginning of the Swedish Pirate Party, we used this mechanism a lot. Whenever there was an article in oldmedia on our issues, we would send an alert phone text to people interested in swarming to the article and making sure our perspective dominated the comment field. In this way, we were able to give a very clear impression of public opinion on anything that touched our areas — an impression that we turned into reality by creating a persistent perception.

Again, most people will match their actions and opinions to be at least compatible with their perception of the public opinion. Control the public perception of who's the winning team, and you *become* the winning team. Therefore, you need some kind of call-to-arms mechanism to quickly relocate your swarm's activity to where people are looking at that exact moment.

 Control perception of who's the winning team, and you become the winning team.

In the postelection evaluation of the European elections in 2009, the Social Democratic party — Sweden's largest party — wrote that their election workers had seen the Pirate Party "on practically every square in the entire country," showing colors, handing out flyers, and talking to passersby. As the party leader, with a hawkeye on our activities and resources, I knew that this statement was very, very far from the objective truth. But it was our competitor's *perception* of reality — a perception that we had *created*. If the election workers of the country's largest party perceived reality like this, a large part of the general population also did.

It's not just that perception is reality. If you can shape perception, you can also *shape reality*. A swarm excels at this.

## MORE WAYS TO TRICK PERCEPTION

In Sweden, there is a political conference every year known as *Almedalen*, going by that name from the general area it takes place in. It doesn't have an obvious equivalent anywhere I've seen — it's just an informal agreement for everybody working in politics (reporters, analysts, PR people, and politicians) to gather for one specific week on a remote island in Sweden. There are some ten thousand people who go there every year, essentially taking over that part of town for a week.

By wearing distinctive clothing — purple, crisp-looking short-sleeve shirts with our logo and the person's last name printed on the back — we were able to get noticed. We had sent seven people to Almedalen one year wearing such shirts, and by the end of the week, people were asking me, "Just how many people did the Pirate Party send here, anyway? I see you everywhere!" The other parties send delegations of hundreds, and yet it was our seven delegates who got noticed because we made it easy for people to notice us in a crowd. The particular shade of purple stood out everywhere, whereas all the other delegates would wear random private clothes, turning them into an indistinct grey mass. (The choice of color was not random: purple is the party color, but it wouldn't have worked nearly as well if the party color had been grey or beige.)

Don't wear beige and blend in. A few visible people can come across as hundreds.

This is also the reason I encouraged activists to buy and wear shirts with the party's color and logo in the streets. We didn't make any money on the shirts. I didn't care about that income stream. What I wanted was to get the colors out there, into the streets of every city and town in the country. Again, perception is reality.

## RESPECTING ANONYMITY

The more information you require about your activists, the fewer activists you'll have. You're certain to have clowns in the organization complaining about your collecting too little data on the people in the swarm, asking you to collect as much data as possible about every volunteer in order to data-mine and find patterns that can be used in various forms of marketing. Kicking people who do this hard in the groin solves the immediate clown problem: everybody in the organization needs to have responsibility for the primary swarm goal, which can't be attained without a large number of activists. Maximizing the number of activists is therefore always the primary subgoal, and scaring away potential activists counteracts this.

It's not just the workload burden of a potential activist typing in his or her name, phone number, mother's maiden name, shoe size at age twelve, and whatever more data over a half-dozen consecutive pages that will make them a nonrecruit — more often than not, it can be the act of identifying themselves in the first place that is the primary deterrent.

Think about it. Your swarm likely strives to achieve some change in the world. Since you're choosing to use a swarm, you're likely up against resource-rich organizations (where the use of a swarm is the most effective way to dropkick them). You will find that there are many people that want to change the status quo that these rich organizations uphold, but you'll also find that a lot of people don't want to sign their name publicly to that aspiration — several of them may even work for the organizations in question, or be suppliers to them, or otherwise dependent on their goodwill. After all, if they are rich in resources, they control a large enough part of society to be able to cause trouble in society for their opponents — their named opponents.

And thinking about it another minute, you *don't need* to know who your activists are. You just need them to talk about the swarm's issues with their friends, show up at rallies, etc. Many will prefer to be anonymous, and honoring that will make the swarm immensely stronger.

In the Swedish Pirate Party, you can sign up as an anonymous activist. We ask for an e-mail address and/or a phone number where you can be texted. Leave at least one of them; both can be anonymous. It works great.

(You will need to know who your officers are, on the other hand, as they become points of contact at some level. But the many-cogs-in-the-machine activists can be completely anonymous if they prefer — and many do.)

## REWARDING THE LONG TAIL

Many organizations, when discussing marketing, ask themselves how they can sell their values to their target group; how they can get people to like them enough to monetize or profit in other intended ways. That is the entirely wrong question to ask, the entirely wrong framing of the problem, and solving that misframed problem will yield counterproductive results in a swarm environment.

The correct question to ask is, "How can we *reward* people for *discussing* our topic (values, politics, services, products)?"

Note that I say *discuss*, not *promote*. There is a world of difference. People are hyperallergic to positive messages that have been vetted or promoted by a suited-and-tied PR department with shiny bling-toothed smiles. It's the worst thing there is, second only to trying to ski through a revolving door. You want to reward people for mentioning your name, no matter whether they like you or not. Again, this is counter to traditional unidirectional marketing of the shove-down-the-throat kind, but goes very well with what we learned in chapter 4 about message diversity and how crucial that diversity is to success and respect.

 The important thing is to get your swarm discussed and mentioned. Reward that.

Many PR departments, as we also learned in chapter 4, are industrial-grade neurotic about having absolute and precise control over the brand. But when you release that control, you can achieve wonders. The same goes for rewarding the long tail — as in, the people who aren't normally seen — for speaking about your swarm or your topics.

In the Swedish Pirate Party, a significant portion of our homepage was devoted to "People blogging about the Pirate Party." Anybody who mentioned the Pirate Party's name in a blog post — no matter in what context — got their blog post highlighted and linked from our front page. This could be accomplished fairly easily with automated processes.

Let's examine what social dynamics this created.

Most bloggers get ten to twenty visitors a day to their blog. This is "the long tail" of bloggers that, frankly, doesn't get a lot of readers at all, compared to the thousand- and million-reader blogs that tend to set the agenda. Nevertheless, these small-scale bloggers are just as sensitive to — and curious about — traffic spikes as the larger blogs.

Imagine you had one of these blogs, your traffic was in the low twenties of visitors a day, and all of a sudden you had a traffic spike of some five hundred visitors when you mentioned the Pirate Party in a blog post. (This was the actual effect of promoting everybody who mentioned us on our well-visited front page.)

What would you think and feel about those sudden numbers if you were a small but aspiring blogger? How would that affect your blogging? More importantly, when you sat down to write your next blog post, what *subjects* would you have in mind for that article?

This is one of the mechanisms behind our becoming the most-discussed party in the entire Swedish blogosphere. When you give up the illusory control of your brand — which you never had anyway — and reward people for discussing you, unconditional of the context, they will *keep* discussing you and your topics, services, or products. That is exactly what you want to happen.

So reward the long tail with attention — that can tip an entire blogosphere toward discussing you, with the exception of the star bloggers, but they're the few and the long tail are the many.

## USING ATTENTION TO BUILD A COMMUNITY

On August 29, 2012, Barack Obama — the president of the United States — did a thirty-minute so-called *AMA* on a site called Reddit. AMA is short for "Ask Me Anything." Anybody in the whole world had an opportunity to ask questions directly and personally to the president of the United States, and he responded to as many as he could during the allocated time.

Some twenty-three thousand people took the opportunity to ask questions directly of the president of the United States. He had time to respond to only ten of them, but did so in a very personal, frank, and candid manner — not just sticking to political questions, but also naming his favorite sports player, talking about how he managed his work/life balance, and discussing beer recipes.

A number of generations into the future, it may be perfectly normal to be able to speak to anybody in the whole world and get responses, including from heads of state — but today, it is most definitely not. This extends to leaders of swarms. People do not expect to get comments and cheers from leaders of political parties or other significant organizations. You can use this nonexpectation to your strong advantage to build a following.

In artistry, this is known as *connecting with fans.* It is the exact same thing, although you need to actively seek out the fans in question rather than just allowing them to speak to you.

When I led the Swedish Pirate Party, as soon as somebody mentioned the party by name on a blog, I would see if I could contribute anything to the discussion (did they ask a question out in the air or wonder aloud about anything?). When somebody mentioned on Twitter or their blog that they had joined the party, I would write a short "Welcome aboard!" signed by me personally. This was easily accomplished with a folder of bookmarks containing search pages across blogs, Twitter, etc.: it was a one-click operation to see if any-thing had appeared that mentioned the party's name.

Still, this blew people's minds. They did absolutely not expect to be personally welcomed by the party leader *in their own space,* that this person *would come to them.* Doing so builds a very strong following and activist base. However, it also requires continuous work. The president of the United States may get away with answering ques-tions for thirty minutes total, but you are not a head of state. You need to search for new activists or potential activists every day, at least once a day, and just acknowledge that you see them — in your own preferred way. While it requires continuous work, it is not really that burdensome — just make sure to have a couple of book-marks with search across blog networks and Twitter for the swarm's name and your own name, and go to those bookmarks once or twice a day.

Attention is reward. Unexpected attention is great reward. Reward people for their interest in your swarm, and show them attention. It works wonders.

 Attention is reward. Unexpected attention is great reward.

In the same manner, engage with people who read what you write. If people ask questions in the comment fields of your columns, articles, or blog posts, engage with them. This is generally not expected, but very appreciated, and builds a strong following. (I've seen people be downright surprised over the fact that I respond to questions they ask me in the comment field of my own columns: "Just ask Rick a question in the comment field; odds are he'll even respond.") This is quite surprising and shows what the current net generation is conditioned to — that people who write publicly lock themselves in an ivory tower and don't want to be talked back to. Come down from the tower and connect with fans, and you'll get a much stronger following, activist base, and swarm.

Also, the *monkey see, monkey do* principle that we discussed in chapters 4 and 7 applies even more when discussing in public and in other people's spaces. People will be rude to you from time to time (after all, your swarm is trying to change the world, which is guaranteed to make some people angry). This will be challenging to your mood and psyche, but you *need* to respond, and you need to be *nice and polite.* You may never turn the person who is rude to you and angry at your values, but you will take every other reader on the site by complete surprise, and *they* will become potential activists in your swarm. Odds are you will even get positive responses from people other than the initial aggressor, written out in cleartext to your nice and polite reply.

Just the other day, I got a comment about this in a discussion forum: "Hey! You can't just go out and be *polite* on the Internet! Who do you think you are!?"

"Monkey see, monkey do" also applies to everybody else in your swarm here, of course. People will behave as you behave on public discussion boards about the swarm's ideas. Teach them to be polite and friendly, no matter how harshly and viciously attacked, and you'll win wonders.

Politics is a spectator sport, and so is arguing your case anywhere on the Internet. As they say in other spectator sports, "win the crowd."

*June 7, 2009, at 10:00 p.m. sharp.*

*I'm at the election night dinner. Where 2006 had been a small restaurant, this is a ballroom. One entire wall of the short end is a screen showing the public service television's election night coverage, including the much-anticipated exit polls.*

*In 2006, there had been one Finnish reporter on location. This time, TV crews are lining one entire long wall. Not just Swedish crews, either — crews from all of Europe are here, much to the surprise of the Swedish crews. I have given preference to ten media outlets for phone calls during the night: Reuters, Associated Press, AFP, BBC, CNN, al-Jazeera, Techdirt, Wired, Numérama, and TorrentFreak. Everybody else will have to be on-site.*

*I'm seated center table and front, as is appropriate for the party leader. There are 150, maybe 200 people here, plus a ton of reporters. Seated close to me are Christian Engström, our list-topper for the election, and Rickard "Richie" Olsson, my longtime friend who was the first to know of the party and is now its CTO. Amelia Andersdotter, the second from top on the pirate ballot, is attending another election dinner in her own part of the country. The countdown to the presentation of exit poll results approaches zero. This is it. People start counting — no, shouting — seconds aloud.*

*TEN, NINE, EIGHT, SEVEN…*

*In a final display of uncertainty, I grab the mike and say over the PA, "Remember that these numbers don't include the advance votes." That uncertainty will prove to be unnecessary within a few seconds.*

*Some thirty cameras are trained on me from the end of the table, in three rows, as the results start coming up on screen. Moderates blah blah, Center party blah blah, Blah party blah blah. Bar after bar comes up. My pulse must be hitting 180 by this point, and I'm just waiting for the verdict.*

*"The Pirate Party. Seven percent."*

*The crowd erupts. The roof lifts. From the end of the table, flashes of light like crazy toward me from the three rows of cameras. The loud joy in the room is so intense you can taste it. My mind races — all this tension built up over three years just releases in an instant. I feel myself putting one hand over my mouth and tears welling up in my eyes as I look at the Pirate Party bar on the exit polls, our election victory secured. Minutes later, that picture of a teary-eyed party leader fronts all newspaper websites in the country.*

*Having seen the optimistic numbers in polls while logically calculating the almost-certain odds, and actually winning seats on election night, turn out to be two completely different experiences. The first was a logical calculation. The second is overwhelming emotion.*

*I realize that I must compose myself and address the people present about our phenomenal success, so I go up on stage to cheers and whistles. I tell my dear colleagues that today marks a day when a new generation starts reclaiming their civil liberties, and how this will send shockwaves around the world, and then bring out a surprise I've prepared. I say, we've all seen our party's polo shirts and jackets with the logo and a function on the back — we've been having uniformlike clothing for recognizability, clothes that have said things like "Piratpartiet, District Lead" or "Piratpartiet, Media Service" on the back for our go-to people. I say that the occasion calls for an entirely new line of clothing, and ask Christian Engström to come on stage.*

*As he comes up on stage, I bring out a fresh, crisp jacket saying "Piratpartiet, Member of European Parliament" on the back, and show it to the crowd. Cheers erupt. "Congratulations, Christian," I say as I hand it to him. The crowd goes wild. "Chris-tian! Chris-tian! Chris-tian!"*

*TV crews form lines to get comments from Christian Engström and me. Once the majority of reporter crews have what they need from me, I finally sit down to eat my dinner. This time, I don't care if it's gone cold while I've been on official duty. As I eat, a curious thought crosses my mind. Sweden has eighteen seats in the European Parliament, but it's being extended to twenty seats two months from this election. Out of the eighteen seats from Sweden, we're projected to get one. So out of curiosity, I start running tonight's numbers on the Election Authority's online simulation as to who will get seats nineteen and twenty two months out, seats also determined in this election — those two people will only take office slightly later.*

*I run the numbers. I blink. I double-check the numbers. I retype them and run them again, getting the same result. I check the numbers again. No, there's no mistake. I smile, grab the microphone, and take to the stage.*

"Dear colleagues," I say, "as you know, we're likely sending Christian to Brussels once the votes have been finally counted. These votes say we're getting a seat in the European Parliament." People cheer. "But Sweden is getting two more seats in the European Parliament in two months, going from eighteen to twenty seats, and those two seats aren't displayed on these results. I just ran the numbers to find out who's going to get seat nineteen and twenty." I smile and look out across the room.

"We're sending Amelia to Brussels, too!"

The crowd erupts. The roof lifts. Again.

# CHAPTER NINE

# Managing Oldmedia

As much as people would like to disrupt the world by going their own way entirely, you cannot change an existing system without also becoming a little part of it in order to change it from the inside. Everybody can change something, but nobody can change everything. Your swarm's focus probably isn't on changing the way oldmedia works, so this is how you deal with them.

When we discuss "oldmedia," the word is in juxtaposition with "new media" (social media), and thus oldmedia refers to any traditional unidirectional, broadcast-message news reporting where people generally do not contribute, discuss, and talk back. Typical examples of oldmedia would be television, radio, and printed newspapers. These oldmedia still maintain a major say in forming public opinion, especially given the digital generational divide, so mastering this playing field is key. However, the reporters of oldmedia are getting their stories through newmedia channels — and this is where the swarm's speed advantage comes into play.

Many organizations who want to be seen in newspapers or television think in terms of "getting them to run our story," and shape their media strategies from there. This is not only ineffective, but counterproductive. Getting your quotes and your swarm's name into oldmedia is really as easy as helping the reporters write a great story: put yourself in the reporters' position, and think about what they would need at a given moment.

For example, assume that something newsworthy breaks on Twitter that relates to your swarm, and your gut feeling tells you that old-media will probably make a published article out of this piece of news. That's when the clock starts. The reporters read the same newsfeeds on Twitter as you do, and the appearance of the tweet is when they start writing the story. What do they need at this exact point in time?

They need comments and quotes on the story to provide diversity to their coverage.

They will take about thirty to forty minutes to write the story draft, and it will publish in sixty. You have thirty minutes to provide your comments and quotes. If you do that, you are helping the reporters write a good and balanced story, and your quotes will get into the oldmedia story being written. The clock is already running: tick, tick, tick.

Getting a press release out in thirty minutes is hard, but completely doable. Press releases are expected to follow certain formats and contain certain keywords. I find that one of the most efficient ways of writing a press release in a swarm is to use an Etherpad or other form of multiplayer notepad, where everybody writes the document at the same time. As long as people are familiar with your swarm and its ideas and line of arguing, the volunteers in the swarm who jump in to help write the press release will create a completely OK set of comments at worst, and brilliant comments at best. We'll be returning later in this chapter to who writes the press releases and why.

You need to practice getting press releases out to aim for about twenty-five minutes from the initial news event to your press release being sent. This is hard, but doable. In the Swedish Pirate Party, the time drilldown was approximately like this:

In the first five minutes from a news event breaking, we had a go or no-go decision on sending a press release about it.

In five minutes more, ten minutes from the newsbreak, we reached agreement on the angle of the press release and the general tone of the quotes from us.

Another ten minutes were needed for writing the actual press release among three to five people, starting from a template. That means we had the raw text ready twenty minutes from the first knowledge of the news.

It took about five minutes more to get three thumbs-ups (a vetting method we used) and to send the finished press release to the press.

These four actions give us twenty-five minutes in total.

 You need to be able to send a press release in 25 minutes, from idea to transmission.

Once a draft is finished, it is very easy to polish it forever while the minutes tick by. Every minute lost in this phase increases the probability that the oldmedia reporter will already have finished writing the story — and once it is published, don't bother sending a press release; the reporters will have moved on to working on another story, and putting your press release in their hands at that point will just irritate.

For transmission to reporters, we use a regular WordPress blog, as people are often familiar with posting articles in WordPress. A special tool picked up anything new posted and mailed it to a long list of reporters, as filtered by the categories set on the article in Word-Press. You can use pretty much any tool, as long as it is familiar to the activists in your swarm, persistent (you need a public-facing archive of press releases — WordPress wins again), and quickly transmits the press release.

So what does a press release look like, and what is its purpose? A press release, in its simplest form, is just mail sent to a reporter. (You will need to maintain a list of reporters writing on topics related to your swarm.) The template we used in the Swedish Pirate Party looked like this:

Press release — organization name — date and time

FOR IMMEDIATE RELEASE

Header

Lead paragraph (opens with location)

Quote

Fact

Quote

Fact

End Quote

For More Information

About the Organization

ENDS

These items have certain specific meanings to them. The words "For Immediate Release" at the top are a key phrase that tells oldmedia that they are allowed to print the story immediately, which will be the case for practically all your press releases. Next, the purpose of the header is to get the reporter to read the rest of the mail, so it need not be a perfect title for the story, just accurate enough and *interesting* enough. The body follows, starting with a lead paragraph that summarizes the story, then quotes and facts interwoven. The "For More Information" part is critical — this must be a phone number and/or e-mail address (or other means of direct contact) where the reporter can get hold of a person for immediate and exclusive quotes.

The press release should read as closely to a finished article as possible. The more the oldmedia reporter can cut and paste, the more work you are doing for them, and the higher the probability of becoming part of the story.

Some would argue that the entire point of the press release is to get a reporter to write an entirely new story. We'll return to this a little later in this chapter, when we talk about avatars of the swarm.

Here's a sample press release:

Press Release — The Swedish Pirate Party — July 2, 2010
FOR IMMEDIATE RELEASE

**PIRATE PARTY: "WE'LL RUN THE PIRATE BAY FROM INSIDE PARLIAMENT"**

**Stockholm, Sweden — The Pirate Party issued a surprise election promise today, saying its future Members of Parliament will run the Pirate Bay from the inside of parliament itself. By doing this, they are invoking parliamen-**

tary immunity against prosecution for political work, giving the Pirate Bay complete legal immunity.

"Today, we are taking bold new steps to protect the next generation of entrepreneurs", says Rick Falkvinge, leader of the Pirate Party. "By protecting the Pirate Bay from torrents of legal shelling, we would send a strong signal to the world that Sweden is at the forefront of next generation's services. Therefore, this is a loud and clear election promise."

By issuing this election promise, the party turns running the Pirate Bay into political work, by definition — and Members of Parliament can never be prosecuted or sued for doing political work in parliament, as part of Sweden's constitution.

"We cannot and will not accept the copyright industry's systematic way of torpedoing our future entrepreneurs," says Falkvinge. "Their legal carpet bombing should be illegal — professional saboteurs are professional criminals, regardless of where they get their paycheck."

The Pirate Bay had trouble finding a stable Internet service provider this spring, before the Pirate Party stepped up to the plate and became the Pirate Bay's new ISP. After that, the copyright lobby stepped back its harassment, not wanting to put the Pirate Party in the spotlight before the elections. Falkvinge comments:

"The Swedish Pirate Party is taking responsibility for Sweden's future economy and entrepreneurship," ends Falkvinge. "We show that not in words, but in personal action. Every day."

**For More Information:**

Rick Falkvinge, phone +46 708 303600

See http://press.piratpartiet.se/ for publicity photos, stock footage, etc.

**About the Pirate Party:**

The Swedish Pirate Party was the largest party in the below-thirty group in the European Elections, taking two seats in the European Parliament, and will be contesting the September 19, 2010, parliamentary elections on all levels. It fights for civil rights and next-generation entrepreneurship.

ENDS

This sample press release, which portrays an authentic event that rendered good coverage in oldmedia in all conceivable languages from English to Thai to Greek to Chinese, leads us to the next point: *be provocative*. If you're not making somebody angry, you're probably not doing anything useful. *Have fun* and make your adversaries angry at the same time: this does not only lead to more activists in the swarm, as we saw in chapters 7 and 8, but it also makes you really enjoy your work in the swarm. Plus, it guarantees you a load of media. Oldmedia just *love* provocative.

Let's take that again, because it is important: if you're not making somebody angry, you're probably not doing anything useful. Don't be afraid of people yelling. That's a sign you're doing something *right*.

 If you're not making somebody angry, you're probably not doing anything useful.

This particular sample press release wasn't time sensitive — you will find that there are four types of press releases in terms of planning ahead:

The first kind is the reactive press release, when you're responding to something that happens and you are providing comments. You should be prepared to send these 24/7, by keeping enough activists in some kind of virtual media room that knows how to handle old-media. If enough activists are there — say, some thirty activists (as per the group size rules we learned in chapter 3) — then enough of them will always be awake at any time of day to deal with incoming events. Trim the response time down to thirty minutes or less, and remember that people will want to polish it to no end, which costs time. Keep the spelling correct and the message good enough; time is of the essence here.

The second kind is when you comment on a large event, the time of which is known in advance, but not its outcome (such as an important court verdict). In this case, reporters will have multiple stories ready to run at a moment's notice — the usual sixty minutes of lead time do not apply. You, too, should have multiple press releases ready to go, up to four different ones for different out-comes. Time to send must be below five minutes in this category, and ideally within 120 seconds. This means that one person must be selecting the appropriate prewritten release, filling in a couple of blanks (such as details from a court verdict), and posting/sending it immediately.

The third kind is when you tell oldmedia about something you will do later in the day, like when you stage rallies or send flowers to adversaries ("if you can't convince them, confuse them"). The timing of this press release depends on your action. If oldmedia have the ability to send photographers to your action, you should send it early in the morning of the day in question, in time for the editorial morning meeting — if sent the night before, it would be an old press release by the morning meeting. In my experience, around 6:30 a.m. is a good time. On the other hand, if oldmedia cannot be expected to send photographers, you are expected to make photos and/or video from the event available yourself, which will vastly increase your chances of becoming a good story (compare the discussion in chapter 4 on filming rallies with a HD camera on a tripod). These kinds of press releases can be written in no rush the day or evening before and scheduled for release (using WordPress or similar) at 6:30 the next morning.

The fourth kind is when you remind oldmedia about something that you're about to do. Reporters are people, and people need reminders when something important is about to happen. For a political party, this could be the election night dinner, where a press release about location, time, and accreditations could be sent fourteen days ahead of the election night, and then followed up with a reminder some seven days ahead.

It should be noted here that there are few instructions here concerning how you can tell oldmedia about what you *think* or *feel* in general, but there are instructions for telling them what you do. Old-media are not *interested* in what people think or feel; they are interested in what people *do*. There is some room for people commenting on what other people do, but there is never editorial room to say what people think without a context of somebody who did something.

(A notable exception to this is opinion pieces, so called op-eds, which we'll return to later in this chapter.)

## OWNING YOUR ISSUE IN OLDMEDIA

A key concept in dealing with oldmedia is "owning the issue." Basically, it means that your swarm needs to be so tightly associated with the issues you drive or things you sell that whenever oldmedia come across a story on the topic, they call you for comments.

 It is strategically crucial that you own your swarm's issue with all or most oldmedia.

This is strategically crucial, and it can literally take years to get into this position if others are also fighting for that particular beachhead on the particular issue. The Swedish Pirate Party quickly owned the issue of file sharing in oldmedia, but it took years for us to own the bigger picture — that of privacy and civil liberties in legislation. Specifically, it took us from January 1, 2006, to June 18, 2008, when we staged unignorable rallies against a new sweeping surveillance law in Sweden.

Ideally, you want to get into a position where reporters of oldmedia call you regularly just to check if there's any story on your topic that hasn't been published yet. We were in this position for a week following the raid on the Pirate Bay on May 31, 2006, as we sat on a ton of material. When you're being called like that and are able to give the reporters stories that haven't been published yet, you're basically in charge of the newsflow on your topic.

## MEDIA BREAKTHROUGHS

Oldmedia won't even mention a new swarm by name until it does something significant. Just existing and having opinions is not interesting. You will likely need to work diligently for several months before hitting an interesting breakthrough to oldmedia — the net is much, much quicker than oldmedia in discovering new talent.

When the oldmedia breakthrough happens, though, you will not miss it. It will quite likely coincide with an activist verticality that we discussed in chapter 7 — when a movement grows dramatically as a result of some big event, that's always interesting to oldmedia. You will be on television every hour on the hour for a week across pretty much all channels, and there will be no end of invitations to submit op-ed articles large and small. (We'll be returning to op-eds shortly.)

## THE GANDHI SCALE IS ACCURATE

Gandhi once said, "First they ignore you, then they ridicule you, then they fight you, then you win." This is eerily accurate in oldmedia's portrayal of any disruptive or provocative swarm.

> "FIRST THEY IGNORE YOU, THEN THEY RIDICULE YOU, THEN THEY FIGHT YOU, THEN YOU WIN."
>
> – *MAHATMA GANDHI*

The results of this can be very counterintuitive. When you have been fighting through months and months of hard work to get any attention, and articles that portray you as stupid clowns start appearing in oldmedia, it is very easy and logical to feel disheartened. You need to know — to logically understand — that being ridiculed is a significant step *forward* from not being mentioned at all, and a necessary stepping-stone on the path to winning. We would talk about G2 articles, G3 articles, and G4 articles — G2 being level two on the Gandhi scale, an article ridiculing your swarm and your efforts.

## WHO WRITES THE PRESS RELEASE?

As mentioned earlier, you will need a media subswarm of thirty people at the most. These people could reside in a chat channel of your choice — Skype, IRC, XMPP, Mumble, etc. — and should ideally be a mix of people that are active during different times of day, so you'll statistically always have at least three people ready to respond to an event with a reactive press release.

This subswarm should be autonomous and have full authorization to speak independently on behalf of the swarm, just like individual activists have, as we discussed in chapter 4 about diversity. If you want a tradeoff, you can create a three-activist rule, that three people in the media subswarm need to approve a press release before sending it. However, named people should never be gatekeepers, as they can be unavailable for a myriad of reasons, and therefore bottlenecks.

One problem with such a group is that media responsibility is seen as a high-profile assignment — read "high-status" assignment — by one type of activists, and such people will tend to get themselves into the media group for the sake of being in the media group, rather than for working efficiently with oldmedia. You will need to make sure that people who become part of this subswarm are not blocking a position for somebody else that you'd rather have there.

## AVATAR FACES OF THE SWARM

This leads us to the question about avatar faces of the swarm. When working with oldmedia, the swarm needs one outward face, and one face only. This would typically be the swarm leader or founder (you). It is important to realize that this is an *avatar* face — it is not you as a person, but a face that represents a larger and very specific movement.

We see this face in the sample press release earlier in this chapter: "Rick Falkvinge, leader of the Pirate Party, says...."

Several swarms have tried to abstain from having this avatar face, and they quickly discover that it works very poorly against oldmedia. Put simply, every swarm needs an avatar — an embodiment of the swarm — to get represented in oldmedia.

Every swarm needs one avatar face – an embodiment of the swarm – for oldmedia.

Very soon after a media breakthrough, some of the activists who joined the media group for the sake of being able to say they're "working with the media" will demand that *they* should be the person speaking in the press release. After all, they wrote it, why shouldn't they be the one speaking in it? (Some would describe such people as attention junkies. While derogatory, it describes the condition rather accurately from a purely lexical standpoint.)

At this point, it becomes important to remember that the function of a press release is to get the swarm's name in oldmedia, and that it is the oldmedia rules that you need to play by. One organization, one face. There are exceptions, but those exceptions are so large and well-established that they won't apply to your swarm.

On the contrary, you need to teach the media subswarm to write quotes and attribute them to you, the swarm leader or founder, for these reasons. If you've taken enough part in the media group and written enough press releases yourself, the subswarm will know the kind of things you say and be able to send out a press release with quotes in your name without needing you as a bottleneck. You'll be amazed at how smart you can sound when you let other people make up the quotes you say without asking you first.

## GETTING FACE TIME: BE WHERE CAMERAS ARE

As much as possible, you will want to be on location where the most important things to your swarm happen. "Sending somebody" is not enough — the avatar faces of the swarm, typically you, have to be at the most important events. There are several reasons for you being there personally.

The first reason is that if you witnessed firsthand what happened, you are able to report on it, discuss it, and debate it in the first person. This is crucial for credibility: saying "I was there, and you weren't" wins major points in any debate. The second reason is that you'll want your own media footage of important events, with the swarm's avatar face in it, to make such footage available as stock cutaways for oldmedia later.

But the third and crucial reason, if there are TV news crews there, is that those TV crews will be looking for some footage worth their while. They will likely have set up their camera well in advance, trimming light and sound, and then doing nothing but waiting for whatever-it-is to happen. If your swarm is seen as owning the issue of what's happening at this location, getting TV time is usually as easy as walking up to the TV crews, introducing yourself, handing over a business card, and saying, "If you'd like me to comment on what's happening here, I'd be happy to do so." Don't be any kind of pushy — media crews hate that — but be friendly and simply tell them that you're here and available.

More often than not, they'll jump at the opportunity of getting your comment right away. After all, it's much-better-spent time for them to get your comments than just wait around and get absolutely nothing produced. The win for you, obviously, is that your comment goes to the cutting board of the TV evening news — and more often than not, a comment of yours makes it to the broadcast, just from you walking up to the TV crews and saying hi.

## SCORING THOSE OP-EDS

An op-ed is usually a full-page print in a newspaper. It is not news reporting, but an opinion piece; it can be regarded as a blog post in oldmedia, and it has quite a bit of reach. (The word "op-ed" has a very simple explanation: it stands for *opposite editorial page,* as op-eds were traditionally printed there.)

Newspapers usually try to get interesting talking points about current events on these pages, and it can be a great way for your swarm to be seen. There are basically four different opportunities for getting an op-ed into a newspaper.

But before we start looking at those four different ways, let's address one thing that's in common between all of them: you never, ever send an op-ed to more than one newspaper in some kind of hope of getting it published in more than one location. Newspapers *hate* people who do that. You pick one paper that you think will have the right reach and audience, and then address that newspaper only. If they decline to publish, you are free to move on to other papers, and only then.

The first kind of opportunity for getting op-eds is when there's something big and public coming up, or an anniversary of some significant event, or anything that prompts a specific subject to be discussed on that date that you know of well in advance. This is typically the easiest route for new players. One to three weeks ahead of the date you aim for, you mail the editorial office and pitch a subject for their op-ed page. You do that by explaining what you want to write about, why you want to write about it on that partic-ular date, and give them the first part of your intended op-ed article, so they get a feel for your message and writing style. Include the subject in the subject line of the mail.

Here's an example from when I successfully pitched an op-ed for the first day of the trial against the operators of the Pirate Bay:

TO: oped@newspaper.com

SUBJECT: The Pirate Bay trial: "Political Trial of the Decade"

DATE: February 9, 2009

Dear Editor,

Considering the trial against the operators of the Pirate Bay that begins in a week, on February 16, I'd like to submit an op-ed with this title and introduction, for publication before the trial, as close to the first date of the trial as possible. Would you find this interesting?

Sincerely,

[signature]

## Political Trial of the Decade

This Monday, the largest political trial of the decade begins in Sweden — probably the largest political trial since the IB trials in the 1970s. In one corner of the ring, we find the Catholic Church, trying to ban the printing press at any cost, this new machine that threatens the monopolies of the Church over knowledge and culture. In the other corner, we find those who have given culture and knowledge to the people. In the jury box, we find the feudal lords who lend their power to the Church, and who are rewarded in turn by the Church telling ordinary people to obey their feudal lords.

Even though the scene above comes from France in the 1500s, the exact same scene will take place in the District Court of Stockholm, beginning on February 16. The power play is identical, the upheaval of structures as large. Only the players are different.

If the editors are interested, as they were with the pitch above, they will respond by asking for a word count and give you a deadline for delivery of the final piece. You need to adhere almost religiously to this word count, and it is usually shorter than you think: you will need to shorten, shorten, and shorten your message again.

Once you're known to the newspapers and you know their desired word count in advance, you could also send your entire article at once, reducing the workload need for a roundtrip. The easier you make it for newspapers, the more they like you.

Your reward for playing by the oldmedia rules is that you get a large audience for your message. You usually don't get paid. Don't expect to get paid, and don't ask. Your payment is exposure of your message to their audience.

The second kind of opportunity for op-eds is when somebody else gets an op-ed published that you vehemently disagree with. This provides an opportunity for a response from you on the op-ed page. Responses are much shorter than the initial op-ed, but it still gets your swarm's name and message out there. You still have to ask for it, and this is somewhat harder to get if you're unknown.

The third kind of opportunity for op-eds is practically impossible to score unless you're already an established player. That opportunity is reactive — as in, submitting the op-ed in response to a large news event that just occurred. Newspapers will welcome op-eds that discuss current events, but usually only from people and organizations who are already well-known. Speed is absolutely essential here — if you can respond in seconds on Twitter when a newspaper asks for an op-ed there, you can still score it. (Most don't ask on Twitter from the editorial oldmedia accounts, but some individual editors do from theirs.)

Finally, during those intense breakthrough moments when you're in the center of attention, it happens that you get requests for op-eds by oldmedia. Always try your utmost to fulfill these requests, keep the word count that is requested, and deliver before the deadline. This sends the message that you're reliable when oldmedia asks you to provide content for them, and will give you more opportunities down the line.

## SET UP A PRESS CENTER

Finally, you'll also need to set up a *press center*. In all simplicity, this is somewhere where reporters can go and download pictures of you for publication, get action shots of the organization's activities, get stock footage from your rallies, and look at an archive of your press releases. (A simple WordPress blog is *excellent* for this purpose, which is another benefit to using WordPress as a press release launcher as described earlier.)

You remember the footage from rallies that we discussed in chapter 4? When we discussed setting up HD cameras on tripods? The results of that need to go into the press center. As does the footage from high-profile events we discussed above, publicity photos, high-resolution images of your logo, and any fact boxes that you want oldmedia to repeat verbatim when they describe your swarm. You'll find that having this available *without asking* means that old-media makes a lot more stories about you, when they can splice in stock footage from your activities into their reporting. If you don't provide such footage…well, they'll make a story about somebody else.

Don't forget to include bios and high-resolution photos of any people you want to profile.

The address to this press center should be at the bottom of every single press release, and it should be as simple as *http://press.your-swarm.org* or *http://www.yourswarm.org/press*.

*September 18, 2011, at 8:00 p.m. in Berlin, Germany.*

*I knew this day had been coming a month ago, when polls had put the German Piratenpartei at 4.5 percent. While that was below the German threshold for parliament, which is at 5 percent, it was close enough to attract all the media spotlights to a newcomer darling, which in turn sky-rocketed their numbers.*

*I've flown down to Berlin to experience that magic moment, and I've rigged up all my cameras to get that fantastic footage that we were too excited to get ourselves in 2009. All footage aside, this is really something that can't be fully communicated — only experienced.*

*I'm at the trendy Ritter Butzke club in Berlin. Some nine hundred people are here, at the Piratenpartei Berlin's election night party. It's not so much a dinner, as the Swedish party had had, as just a wild party. Almost nobody recognizes me, and I kind of like that — it's the ideas that are powerful, and not me as a person.*

*I get in, pick a quiet corner that overlooks the crowd, and wait for the exit polls that arrive at 8:00 p.m. sharp. As they approach, I rig my cameras on tripods to catch the magic moment. In large parts, it's a repeat from our election victory in Sweden in 2009.*

## TEN, NINE, EIGHT, SEVEN...

*As the television presenters start giving the numbers of the exit polls, the crowd falls reverently silent. Not speaking German, I don't hear the nuances, I just hear party name acronyms and percentages. The people cheer a little as their favorite disappointment, the FDP, only gets 2 percent and falls out of Parliament. Then, suddenly, people listen up intensely for a fraction of a second as their party name is called.*

*"Piratenpartei, 8.5 percent."*

*Arms go up in the air. The deafening cheers lift the roof. People are hugging each other everywhere. Some people are crying with joy.*

*I try to maintain composure for the remainder of the scene, and manage to get the rest of it before I turn off my cameras — but I can't help it, I feel the tears coming. I pack the cameras and seek out a quiet corner for a while to let my tears of joy come freely — I was not prepared for this emotion, this overwhelming joy at the success of our sister party, the first success outside of the cradle of Sweden.*

*As I regain composure, I hover a bit around the stage to find some people I know, and before long, I run into people that I know from international pirate meetings. They insist that I say a few words on the stage. While this is their victory, I am happy to take part in celebrations, so I step up on stage and use what little German I know.*

*"Friends, colleagues, pirates," I say in the best German I can muster, "I am Rick Falkvinge. I am the founder of the Swedish and first Pirate Party." Cheers erupt. The roof lifts. I feel tears welling up again.*

*I tell them that they just became the heroes of a generation, and that this election victory won't just be in the Berliner Zeitung (a Berlin paper), and it won't just be in Der Spiegel (a German paper). Tomorrow, this victory will be in the Wall Street Journal, al-Jazeera, and the Hindu Times. I don't know it yet, but I am wrong about the "tomorrow" part. News about the Piratenpartei's Berlin victory is already published in those papers, and many more worldwide.*

*During the night, I speak to reporters from all over the world. While this is the German Piratenpartei's victory, many of them are busy just celebrating. Nobody can say they deserve anything less.*

*Later, Swedish Public Television would use footage from that night with me speaking at the Piratenpartei's election night party in a documentary about the copyright monopoly, and subtitle it "If this country has a rogue face, it would be this one." When I see it, I laugh so hard I fall off my chair.*

# CHAPTER TEN

# Beyond Success

**In many ways, success can be harder to handle than failure, because it sets expectations most people have never felt. These are some of the most important experiences on how to not make a wild success crash on its maiden flight into a painful failure.**

As your swarm starts to rise to prominence and success, you personally will invariably do so, too. This was probably never a goal of the swarm as such, but it is the way oldmedia's logic works — they need a face to associate with every movement or organization, and if the movement is successful, so is that particular face.

The danger lies in not realizing that people will regard everything you say as having much more weight than you place on it yourself at the time you say it. If your swarm is political, anything you do — or don't do — will be interpreted as a political statement, everything from your choice of groceries to your pick of vacation resort. Anything you say will be interpreted as a suggestion for legislation. This translates into any other type of swarm, too — the effect doesn't limit itself to political swarms.

To take an example, you could easily see somebody mildly drunk in a sports bar, a half-empty glass of beer in hand, shouting angrily at the football game on screen, and muttering, "What this game needs is a bullet to the referee's head" under his breath to himself. Nobody takes such a statement literally, because of the situation it was uttered in and the person it was uttered by.

Now, imagine the exact same sentence uttered by the prime minister or president in the same bar and situation, but with reporters nearby — or for that matter, anybody with a blog nearby. It would take literally minutes before an oppositional blogger had an article out about how the prime minister wants to reinstate a barbaric death penalty for unsuitable sports professionals, and "has been overheard planning to introduce a bill about it in the near future." Cue the inevitable shitstorm.

This is the situation you'll find yourself in quite rapidly as your swarm starts to gain attention and success, and it will place great demands on you to start saying only what you really mean. While we tend to think we already do this, we say many things in closed company that are understood in the context of that company to not be meant literally. Those get-out-free cards are gone once you've been on the news a couple of times. Reporters and other people will start asking, "Did you really mean that?" and you will respond with a confused "But wait, I didn't mean it that way" and immediately risk coming across as a backpedaling second-rate politician on the evening news. You want to avoid this.

The simplest way to avoid it is to be nice to all people, even to your adversaries. Doing so will not just benefit the culture of the swarm, where you lead by example and show people that being excellent to each other is the way to behave, but it will also catch your adversaries completely off guard. This is a good thing: "If you can't convince them, confuse them." You don't have to agree with them — you just have to disagree nicely and politely.

## THE DAY AFTER SUCCESS

In the entertainment business, they say that no time is as tough as the year *after* that year when you were the hottest thing of the town. This applies to every swarm as well. When we've been on a slowly upward trajectory for a couple of years, we tend to believe that any dings — any level-ups — are permanent ascensions to a new base level of popularity, acceptance, and visibility.

That is an illusion. Moreover, it is an illusion everybody in the swarm gets afflicted by, from the founder down to the individual activist.

Everybody in society is constantly fighting for visibility. Getting visibility is hard. Keeping it is even harder, for other people will seek to take it for their own causes.

The problems arrive when everybody in the swarm takes for granted that the current popularity, visibility, sales, or whatever your measure of success is will keep on for the next year or two. When that happens, they will stop working extrovertedly, and start fighting between themselves for all the riches and resources and fame that they see coming the swarm's way on the expected continued success: everything from lavish jobs to expensive toys to personal visibility. As an inevitable result, the swarm's success will collapse in months — and it won't be a temporary glitch, it will be a deep structural problem based on faulty expectations of individual reward that takes time and effort to repair.

Getting visibility in society is hard.
Keeping it is even harder.

As the founder, it is your job to explain that when things appear to be at their peak, all those lavish jobs and expensive toys are farther away than ever. At that point in time, the swarm has two of its toughest challenges ever to overcome — to remain steadfast on the extroverted track, despite the distracting glimmering riches on the horizon, and the fact that the visibility and success will fade even if the swarm continues exactly on its current course of action, and this can be a very tough thing to face emotionally.

The Swedish and German Pirate Parties both fell for this predictable but treacherous mechanism. When the Swedish Pirate Party gained two seats in the European Parliament in 2009, with 7 percent of the votes, everybody felt that the parliamentary elections of the next year were practically a done deal. In reality, the race for those elections had only just started, and when people started forming factions for resources to mark their stake in how all the riches would be divided, the race was already lost. The German Pirate Party was the shooting star of 2011, winning a sensational 9 percent in the Berlin elections, and quickly climbing to 13 percent in the national polls, enough for a full eighty seats in Parliament (out of 622). At this point, unless actively countered, people will start seeing inevitable money and resources everywhere, and will start fighting for the five-hundred-or-so jobs that would be the outcome of such an election result. As of today's writing one year later, the German Piratenpartei is polling at 3 percent, below the 5 percent parliamentary threshold for entry, with about nine months to go until the election.

This type of downfall is reversible and repairable, but it takes time and a lot of organizational and personal anguish to do so. Basically, once this downward spiral has set in, the swarm needs to bottom out at a failing level before people realize there aren't any riches, at which point the repairs can start. This is painful for everybody involved. So keep the swarm on track, and do remind them of that saying in the entertainment business: no time is as tough as the year after the year you're hot — and that year will come around, as certainly as the calendar tells you it will.

## GOING INTERNATIONAL

If your swarm's goals are of an international nature, you will very quickly see copycat movements in other countries, as activists there realize that your recipe for changing the world would work in their country, too. The Pirate Party has spread organically to seventy countries as of this writing, founded by me as an individual person on January 1, 2006.

There are basically three ways to handle an internationalization. The first is to ignore the people you inspire altogether, leaving them to their own devices, which is a bad idea from all conceivable angles. The second, better way is to lend as much energy and resources as you can to the international copycat movements without sacrificing the operational capability of your own swarm: provide the software you have already developed, experiences you've drawn, logotypes and press materials, and so on. Before long, experiences and promotional materials will start flowing in both directions as the swarms in other countries mature.

The third way is to aspire to lead *all* countries' movements, just as you led the first country. It is likely that people in the new countries will agree to this, but it presents considerable cultural challenges.

Just because you understand a language, that doesn't mean you understand what people are trying to say.

To give two examples, when I was working for a company based in the United States, I casually said "good luck" to an American manager who was heading off to negotiations. To somebody in Sweden, this is a friendly, casual expression on par with "godspeed" or "best of winds." To somebody coming from a proper United States context, however, it has a distinct undertone of "because you're going to need it" that I was completely unaware of when saying it. The careful translation of words isn't enough to understand what you're actually saying — or rather, what the person you're talking to is hearing.

The second example is when I was in Brazil, and after a day of meetings, the crowd agreed to meet at 9:00 p.m. at a certain bar. Coming from northern Europe, to me, that statement means that you step through the door of that bar at 8:58 or 8:59 p.m., take thirty to forty-five seconds to locate your colleagues in the bar, and join them with some fifteen to thirty seconds to spare before the second hand on the watch passes the full hour of 9:00 p.m.

I had a feeling it didn't mean the same thing in Brazil, and I've learned it's better to ask once too often, so I asked, "So…9:00. Does that mean, like, 10:00?" Everybody laughed at my question, except for one person in the group who had grown up in the United States and moved to Brazil at an adult age. With his background, he understood that my question was actually serious. "Yes, Rick," he said as laughter subsided, "about 10:00. Or maybe 11:00." To the

Brazilians, saying "9:00" was just an arbitrary number for meeting some time in the evening — my counterquestion of "10:00" made absolutely no sense to them, as 10:00 was as arbitrary and meaningless a number as "9:00" had been.

These are just examples of everyday misunderstandings that will happen when you try to lead across cultures. Those nuances don't come with learning a language, but you need to understand them in order to lead effectively. I would argue that it's superhuman to understand more than two or three cultures to the depth necessary for leading a swarm in that culture, as a swarm is very informal by its nature.

If you do insist on leading all countries formally, I would argue that you need one or two people in every country to act as your local deputies, and that you spend a lot of time understanding the cultural differences in resolving any actions and paths ahead. Your preconceptions *will* be a mismatch for other cultures, and you won't even be aware of the differences unless you take active steps to identify them.

At some point, an international support group will form by itself with the self-appointed task of coordinating the international versions of your swarm between countries, languages and cultures. At that point, it will be up to you whether you decide to step up and try to lead the international efforts, or keep leading your national swarm. I would recommend that you stay and lead your national swarm for at least as long as it takes to have its first major success.

I led the Swedish Pirate Party for its first five years, putting two people in the European Parliament on June 7, 2009, which sent political shockwaves around the entire world. After that success, the proof of concept was there, and there was a success blueprint in place. That was the major success necessary. After that, there was no further doubt in the world that this could actually be pulled off.

## DON'T SHOOT FOR THE MOON

In closing, it is possible for one person to set out to change the world and succeed. Other people hold no genetic advantage over you — there is nothing inherent to say that their position is superior to yours and that you can't succeed. Quite to the contrary, it is much a matter of attitude.

No matter whether you believe that you can or cannot change the world, you are probably correct.

There is nothing taking place within the laws of physics that you cannot accomplish. Don't shoot for the moon in changing the world — that has already been done by somebody else. Shoot for Mars! Build a Mars colony. That's perfectly doable by somebody determined who builds a swarm to support the initiative.

 Don't shoot for the moon! That's been done already. Aim higher. Go for Mars!

Just like with any idea to change the world, if you approach it like a project, you can execute it like a project. "Let's see. We need two dozen volunteer rocket scientists, maybe a dozen metallurgists, a couple of people crazy enough to mix rocket fuel in their back yard...." When you know what it takes to get from A to B, the rest is just execution and inspiration. Therefore, the first step is to tell the world that you're going to go from A to B, and say what you think it takes to do so, as we saw in chapter 2. A hurdle is never impossible once you know exactly what it looks like — only when you fear its height because you've never taken the effort to find out how difficult it actually is to climb.

Of course, your initial estimates of what it takes may be off the mark. They may not even be in the correct ballpark. But in order to discover that, you must put a stake in the ground and start executing the project, and work by trial and error. As we've seen, iteration speed is key. Try, improve, adapt, try again. Iterate, iterate, iterate. You will likely be surprised yourself at how quickly plans materialize and self-adjust once you get expertise from various fields involved in the project.

 Put a stake in the ground and work by trial-and-error. Iterate, iterate, iterate.

The Swedish Pirate Party set out to go from nothing to getting elected in eight months. We discovered many hurdles along the way, and assessed and passed them just as quickly, working as a swarm where anybody could contribute expertise freely. While we were disappointed with our first election result of 0.6 percent, everybody else was very impressed and had never expected that. The following election brought us into the European Parliament, so "getting elected" became a project executed at one-half of the time of the previous major political movement and at less than 1 percent of the cost of the competition.

The laws of physics are your only limit. (Unless you're a theoretical physicist, in which case not even those laws may be a hard barrier.)

You want to teach two billion people how to read and write, ending illiteracy in the world? Completely doable.

> CAN YOU IMAGINE WHAT I WOULD DO IF I COULD DO ALL I CAN?
>
> *— SUN TZU, "THE ART OF WAR"*

You want to provide artificial light and heating to a billion people in developing countries? Or clean water? A swarm can make it happen.

How about teaching five billion people rational thinking and scientific approach, in an attempt to end religious conflicts? Totally within grasp.

Don't shoot for the moon. Shoot for Mars!

## FINAL WORDS

In my worldwide presentations, I describe how everybody can change the world if he or she is passionate about a specific change, and that change is tangible, credible, inclusive, and epic enough to attract a swarm.

Whether your dream is to end illiteracy and teach two billion people to read, or you want to take humanity to Mars, the principles are the same.

Change doesn't just happen, I say.

Somebody always *makes* it happen.

The final words of this book will therefore be the same words that close my presentations and workshops about cost efficiency in management and volunteer activism:

Do *you* want to be that person?

# WORKSHOPS AND KEYNOTES

The author offers competitive workshops for corporate and governmental environments, aimed at any management who desires training in swarm methodologies and their corresponding agility and cost-efficiency, as described in this book.

Workshops start at the half-day level and are also available as in-depth multi-day trainings.

The author can also provide keynotes at commercial and non-profit conferences on the topic. Examples and references can be found at *http://falkvinge.net/keynotes*.

*See http://falkvinge.net/contact* for contact information.

# ACKNOWLEDGMENTS

As usual, when writing a book, there are many people who serve to inspire, to assist, to proofread, and to periodically kick the author hard enough to actually get a book finished. I'd like to thank these people for their contributions to putting this book in your hands — in alphabetical order, mostly to spare me the social dilemma of sorting my helpful friends and colleagues in any *other* order:

Anna Troberg
Arthur Doohan
Brandon Proia
Christian Engström
Cristina Andersson
Gefion Thürmer
Kaj Arnö
Karl Fogel
Mika Sjöman
Morgan Andréason
Rickard Olsson
Troed Sångberg

The imagery from the TV broadcast in Berlin was kindly provided by Simon Stützer (CC-BY-SA).

# INDEX